First Edition

Common Core
Support Coach

TARGET Reading
Comprehension 5
Assessments

Common Core Support Coach, Target: Reading Comprehension, First Edition, Assessments, Grade 5
T228NAA

ISBN-13: 978-1-62362-019-6

Cover Design: Q2A/Bill Smith
Cover Illustration: Scott Balmer

Triumph Learning® 136 Madison Avenue, 7th Floor, New York, NY 10016

Contents

Read the story and answer the questions that follow.

Another Silly Idea

1   As I disembarked from the train, I didn't <u>recognize</u> her at first, even as she rushed over to me, shouting, "Anna!"

Then, I glimpsed her parents, Mr. and Mrs. Ramirez, idling at the curb and looking pretty much as they always did. But could this girl with a short, stylish haircut really be my best friend, Luisa?

"Hey," I said, surprised to hear how soft my voice sounded, hardly able to look Luisa in the eye. I suddenly felt ashamed about my tattered and threadbare jeans. They were no different from the scruffy jeans I wore all the time, even before Luisa had moved away to the city. But now, standing next to her in her cute skirt and striped tights, I felt unkempt and all wrong.

I continued to feel all wrong all day. First, we had lunch at a Chinese restaurant. Luisa used the chopsticks with ease, but despite her patient instructions, I was just too uncoordinated. Then we went to her house. I would have preferred to go outside, go for a walk around her neighborhood, and reminisce about how we used to have so much fun barreling through the woods, but Luisa was more interested in holing up at home. She said it was too frigid to go meandering around. I was <u>bewildered</u>. We used to while away the hours out in the woods behind our homes even when the air felt arctic. When had Luisa decided that she didn't like the cold?

5   Instead, we retreated to Luisa's bedroom, where she had a big poster of Caitlyn Casey hung over her bed and where I was made to endure listening to Caitlyn Casey's music all afternoon. Or maybe we listened to the music for just an hour or two, which felt like all afternoon because it was so mundane. I was starting to wonder whether it had been a good idea to visit Luisa in the city in the first place. Maybe she wasn't even my friend anymore, let alone my best friend.

Meanwhile, Luisa kept mentioning a "surprise" and that she couldn't wait until I found out about the "surprise," too. I, however, *could* wait because I was anxious. What if the surprise was something as enjoyable as Caitlyn Casey's music, meaning not at all enjoyable?

Finally, Mrs. Ramirez yelled for us downstairs. "Girls, I have a surprise for you," she said. "Although really, it's only a surprise for Anna. Luisa already knows what it is."

"Tickets to see Caitlyn Casey tonight!" Luisa interrupted, leaping and hollering with anticipation.

"Great!" I said, pretending to be excited, too. But when we went back upstairs to get ready to go, I couldn't help myself. I blurted out, "Since when do you care so much about Caitlyn Casey?"

10   Luisa stared at me. It was as if she was going to cry.

"I'm sorry." I sighed. "It's just that you've changed. You've gotten all weird and different."

"Me?" Luisa said. "Weird and different? What about you? Since when do you care so much about horses?"

"Horses?"

"Yeah, horses. It's all you've talked about today."

15   I hadn't noticed, but it was true; I was acting the same as Luisa. "I guess since you moved. You would like riding, too, though, I think. I wish …" I sighed. "You really want to go hear this singer, Casey whatever her name is, don't you?"

Luisa nodded, and I started to laugh. "You know, I guess nothing's changed," I said. "Aren't I always going along with your silly ideas?"

Luisa started to laugh, too. "Yeah, and you're always finding out that my silly ideas are pretty good ideas."

"Well, I'm not so sure about that this time," I said.

"You'll see!"

1. Which detail would most likely NOT be included in a summary of this story?

   A. Luisa becomes more interested in pop stars.

   B. Anna arrives in Luisa's town by train.

   C. Luisa moves to a different town.

   D. Anna always goes along with Luisa's silly ideas.

2. The word <u>recognize</u> is based on the Latin root *cogn,* meaning "to know." Based on this information, you can conclude that <u>recognize</u> in paragraph 1 means

   A. to feel or care.

   B. to notice or see.

   C. to learn or understand.

   D. to identify or remember.

3. According to the beginning of the story, what is one difference between Anna and Luisa?

   A. Anna generally cares less about her appearance.

   B. Anna generally has less to say than Luisa.

   C. Anna generally has trouble showing her feelings.

   D. Anna generally stays much closer to home.

4. Based on the context in paragraph 4, you can conclude that the word <u>bewildered</u> means

   A. lost.

   B. chilly.

   C. confused.

   D. disappointed.

5. How does Anna's home MOST LIKELY compare with the setting of this story?

    A. It is colder.

    B. It is not in a city.

    C. It is more exciting.

    D. It is in a different country.

6. Based on the conclusion of the story, you can tell that Anna

    A. does not like music.

    B. has a good sense of humor.

    C. thinks that Luisa has only bad ideas.

    D. wants to be more like Luisa.

7. Write a summary of "Another Silly Idea." Include important details from the story in your summary.

_____

_____

_____

_____

Read the story and answer the questions that follow.

Missing Roger

1   Everything changed when Roger left home and traveled far away to college; for one thing, the house seemed strangely quiet. Samuel couldn't figure out why it seemed so quiet because Roger was always reading and was the quietest person Samuel knew. Then Samuel realized that the lack of noise was due to the fact that he had no one to talk to except his parents. And they were different, too. It was as though they had suddenly realized that they had another son whom they could trouble about homework, grades, eating, sleeping, and anything and everything having to do with his humdrum life.

"Don't you want to attend college like your brother?" they'd <u>exclaim</u> if they deemed that his schoolwork didn't meet their suddenly high expectations.

"College is years away! Stop worrying!" he'd retort, but of course they kept on worrying, as if it were their only purpose in life. Samuel started counting down the days until Roger would come back home for the holidays.

But even when Roger returned home that December, things remained different. The days were just as quiet because Roger had exams in January and so spent all his time studying. He wasn't even asked to mind the store, as he had been doing since he was in middle school.

5   "Don't you worry about the store," Mr. Perry said to Roger. "We've been taking care of the store just fine since you went to college, and we can keep taking care of it just as well now. You just worry about your exams."

And Roger did indeed seem worried, and tired, too. So Samuel left him to his books and felt even lonelier than ever.

Then one evening, after staring at the same algebra problem for ten minutes, Samuel decided to ask Roger for help with his homework. He knocked on Roger's bedroom door.

"Hey," Roger said, letting him in and clearing a space for him on the bed. He took a look at Samuel's homework. "Oh, this stuff," he said. "I remember hating this stuff, too, when I was your age."

"Fractions?" Samuel said. "You hated fractions?"

10   Roger grinned. "Sure. Doesn't everyone hate fractions?"

Samuel had seen Roger's math textbook, which included fractions that looked more complicated than anything that Samuel had ever thought possible. "But I thought you liked math."

"I do. But I didn't always."

This was news to Samuel. "Really? Why'd you change your mind?"

"It gets more interesting later on. Doing math is like putting together a puzzle. You'll see."

15   Roger showed Samuel how to solve the problem that had stumped him, and then he watched while Samuel did the next few problems on his own. "You've got it," he said.

"Thanks," said Samuel. "I know it's math homework, but … well, this was fun. Can I do the rest of my homework here? I'll be real quiet. After this, I just have some reading to do."

"Sure thing," said Roger. "Actually, I'd really like that. I miss you. Plus, it's been pretty lonely around here since I've gotten home."

"Lonely for you? What about for me?" Samuel told Roger all about the quiet around the house and the <u>constant</u> worrying and nagging of their parents.

"Sounds as if they've been lonely, too. And it sounds as if I've been spending too much time studying. I'll tell you what. Why don't we take Mom and Dad out to a movie or something?"

20   "Tomorrow night? And we can go out for pizza before?"

"Sounds as if we have a plan!"

8. Which of the following is the BEST summary of this story?

   A. Two brothers disagree about math.

   B. Two brothers do homework together.

   C. Two brothers find ways to be less lonely.

   D. Two brothers lose their friendship with each other.

9. The word exclaim is based on the Latin root *clam,* meaning "to shout." Based on this information and the context in paragraph 2, how do Samuel's parents feel when they exclaim things to him?

   A. upset

   B. threatened

   C. misunderstood

   D. surprised

10. Based on the context in the story, you can conclude that the word constant in paragraph 18 means

    A. sad.

    B. loud.

    C. ongoing.

    D. mixed up.

11. How are Roger and Samuel similar?

    A. They are both annoyed by their parents.

    B. They both think of math as doing a puzzle.

    C. They both enjoy the other's company.

    D. They both spend all of their time studying.

12. Which BEST describes the setting of the story?

    A. a college dorm room

    B. a busy and crowded house

    C. an apartment in the middle of the city

    D. a quiet and lonely house

Use "Another Silly Idea" and "Missing Roger" to answer questions 13 and 14.

13. What theme do the stories share?

    A. Even though people's lives change, some things stay the same.

    B. Friends can disagree about some things, but they still remain friends.

    C. Friends must make compromises in order to be happy.

    D. Even good people can make bad choices.

14. Explain how the characters in both stories solve their problems. What is similar in how they solve their problems? Use details from the stories to support your answer.

_____

_____

_____

_____

Read the poem and answer the questions that follow.

A Patch of Old Snow
by Robert Frost

There's a patch of old snow in a corner
That I should have guessed
Was a blow-away paper the rain
Had brought to rest.

5   It is <u>speckled</u> with grime as if
Small print <u>overspread</u> it,
The news of a day I've forgotten —
If I ever read it.

1. According to the poem, how is the patch of old snow like a newspaper?

   A. Both get blown around by the wind.

   B. Both tell the speaker about the weather.

   C. The snow is as old as a newspaper.

   D. The dirt on the snow resembles print on paper.

2. The word <u>speckled</u> in line 5 means

   A. lost.

   B. smelly.

   C. spotted.

   D. printed.

3. Read this entry from a dictionary.

   o•ver•spread ('ō-vər-spred) *verb.* to spread over or cover

   How many syllables are in the compound word <u>overspread</u> in line 6?

   A. two

   B. three

   C. four

   D. five

4. In the first six lines, the speaker describes a patch of old snow. In the last two lines he

   A. tells about his day.

   B. explains what happened to the snow.

   C. describes a newspaper.

   D. shares his thoughts about the snow.

5. According to line 7, what day has the speaker MOST LIKELY forgotten?

   A. the day before

   B. the day when the snow was new

   C. the day he read the newspaper

   D. the day he wrote the poem

6. Which lines of the poem rhyme?

   A. lines 1 and 3

   B. lines 2 and 4

   C. lines 1 and 4

   D. lines 2 and 3

7. How does the patch of old snow in the corner relate to the old and forgotten newspaper?

_____

_____

_____

_____

Read the poem and answer the questions that follow.

A Vagabond Song

by Bliss Carman

There is something in the autumn that is native to my blood—
Touch of manner, hint of mood;
And my heart is like a rhyme,
With the yellow and the purple and the crimson keeping time.

5   The scarlet of the maples can shake me like a cry
Of bugles going by.
And my lonely spirit thrills
To see thc frosty <u>asters</u> like a smoke upon the hills.

There is something in October sets the gypsy blood astir;
10   We must rise and follow her,
When from every hill of flame
he calls and calls each vagabond[1] by name.

[1] a homeless wanderer

8. In lines 3 and 4, the speaker compares the effect of autumn on her heart with

   A. music.

   B. a flag.

   C. a clock.

   D. a parade.

9. Read this entry from a dictionary.

   bu•gle ('byü-gəl) *noun.* a brass wind instrument that is similar to a trumpet but without keys or valves

   Which best describes the pronunciation of <u>bugles</u> in line 6?

   A. accent on the first syllable; second syllable sounds like *gulls*

   B. accent on the first syllable; second syllable sounds like *fools*

   C. accent on the second syllable, which sounds like *gulls*

   D. accent on the second syllable, which sounds like *fools*

10. In lines 5 and 6, what does the comparison of the scarlet of the maples with the cry of bugles show?

    A. the speaker's fear

    B. the speaker's excitement

    C. the speaker's sadness

    D. the speaker's feeling left out

11. From the context in the poem, you can conclude that <u>asters</u> in line 8 must be a kind of

    A. fire.

    B. snow.

    C. plant.

    D. mountain.

12. How does the third stanza of the poem compare with the others?

   A. It tells about the coming winter, whereas the others tell about autumn.

   B. It describes autumn after the leaves fall, whereas the others tell about autumn colors.

   C. It explains why the speaker dislikes nature, whereas the others celebrate nature.

   D. It sums up the speaker's ideas, whereas the others are more descriptive.

13. Which word in the third stanza gives a context clue for the meaning of <u>vagabond</u>?

   A. October

   B. gypsy

   C. flame

   D. name

14. Describe the speaker's feelings about autumn. Use details from the poem to support your answer.

   _____

   _____

   _____

   _____

Read the drama and answer the questions that follow.

A Cake for Mamsie

adapted from Five Little Peppers and How They Grew
by Margaret Sidney

CAST OF CHARACTERS

POLLY PEPPER
MRS. PEPPER, or "MAMSIE"
JOEL PEPPER
DAVID PEPPER
PHRONSIE PEPPER
BEN PEPPER
GRANDMA BASCOM
MRS. BEEBE

Scene 1

SETTING: *The kitchen of a small, rather shabby rural home in 1800s America. The kitchen features a large, old, cranky black stove and, to one side, a table large enough to seat a family of six. It is afternoon and growing dark. Mrs. Pepper, or "Mamsie," as her children call her, has just finished making a coat. Her oldest daughter, ten-year-old Polly, is helping her pull basting threads out of the coat so that they can be used again. The younger children, Joel, David, and Phronsie, are playing quietly.*

1   POLLY: Oh dear! I do wish we could have more light—just as much as we want!

MAMSIE: (*winding threads on a spool*) You don't need any light to see these threads. Take care, Polly, you broke that. Thread's dear now.

POLLY: Everything's expensive now, it seems to me! I wish we could have ever and ever so many candles, as many as we wanted. I'd light them all at once!

MAMSIE: Yes, and go dark all the rest of the year. Folks who do so never have any candles.

5   JOEL: How many would you have, Polly?

POLLY: Oh, two hundred! I'd have two hundred, all in a row!

JOEL: Two hundred candles! My whockety! What a lot!

POLLY: Don't say such dreadful words, Joel. It isn't nice.

JOEL: It isn't worse than to wish you'd got things you haven't. I don't believe you'd light all the candles at once.

10 POLLY: Yes, I would too! Two hundred of them, if I had a chance, all at once—so there, Joey Pepper!

DAVID: (*sighing*) Why, it would be just like heaven, Polly! But wouldn't it cost money, though?

POLLY: I don't care how much money it cost, we'd have as much light as we wanted, for once!

MAMSIE: Mercy! You'd have the house afire! Two hundred candles! Whoever heard of such a thing!

PHRONSIE: Would they burn?

15 POLLY: (*to Phronsie*) Burn? (*to Mamsie, as she places the coat, now finished, on her mother's lap*) There, that's done now, Mamsie dear! (*picking up Phronsie to spin her around*) I guess they would, Phronsie pet. (*She sets Phronsie down and begins to prepare for supper by pulling the table over to the middle of the kitchen.*)

PHRONSIE: (*clasping her hands in delight*) Then, I do so wish we might, Polly, oh, just this very one minute!

(*The door opens, and eleven-year-old Ben steps into the kitchen. The family greets him warmly.*)

BEN: It's just jolly to get home! Is supper ready, Polly?

POLLY: Yes, just about!

(*The children lay the cloth on the table and set out the dishes and bread and so on, and the family sits down for supper. As they pass around the dishes, Phronsie speaks.*)

PHRONSIE: Sometime, we're going to be awful rich. We are, Ben, truly!

20 BEN: (*pretending <u>astonishment</u>*) You don't say so, Chick!

PHRONSIE: Yes, we are really, Bensie, very dreadful rich!

BEN: (*casting a glance toward Polly*) I wish we could be rich now, then, in time for Mamsie's birthday.

POLLY: I know! Oh dear, if we only could celebrate it!

MAMSIE: I don't want any other celebration than to look round on you all. I'm rich now, and that's a fact!

25 POLLY: (*whispering to Ben*) Well, I don't care. Let's try and get a celebration, somehow, for Mamsie!

BEN: (*also whispering*) How are you going to do it?

POLLY: (*whispering*) Oh, I know, I know the very thing! Let's make her a cake, a big one, you know, Grandma Bascom will tell me how. Although—you know we've only got brown flour, and no eggs or raisins.

BEN: (*whispering and looking toward the old black stove*) And the stove'll act like everything, tomorrow! I know it will, and then what'll you do?

POLLY: (*looking fiercely at the old black stove*) It shall not! And if it does, I'll shake it, the mean old thing!

1. What inference can you make about the time period of the drama?

   A. It takes place before many people had electricity in their homes.

   B. It takes place before people had kitchens in their homes.

   C. It takes place during World War II, when people had to ration supplies.

   D. It takes place during colonial times.

2. Based on their conversation about candles, which is the BEST description of Mamsie and Polly?

   A. Whereas Mamsie is wise, Polly tends to be foolish.

   B. Whereas Mamsie is practical, Polly is imaginative.

   C. Whereas Mamsie has little sense of humor, Polly likes to have fun.

   D. Whereas Mamsie likes her home, Polly is very unhappy with it.

3. The word astonishment includes the Latin suffix -ment, which forms nouns from verbs. Based on this information, you can conclude that astonishment means

   A. surprise.

   B. confusion.

   C. make believe.

   D. the opposite.

4. Which quotation BEST supports the inference that the Pepper family does not have a lot of money?

   A. "Folks who do so never have any candles."

   B. "It isn't worse than to wish you'd got things you haven't."

   C. "Everything's expensive now, it seems to me!"

   D. "I wish we could be rich now, then, in time for Mamsie's birthday."

5. Based on this scene, you can conclude that one of the themes of this play is the importance of

   A. getting rich.

   B. birthday celebrations.

   C. caring for one's family.

   D. making wishes.

6. Which sentence BEST describes this scene?

   A. It focuses on the setting of the story.

   B. It introduces the characters and conflict.

   C. It tells about the theme without involving much plot.

   D. It suggests how the Pepper family will solve their problems.

7. What does Mamsie mean when she says, "I'm rich now, and that's a fact!"? Use details from the passage to support your answer.

   _____

   _____

   _____

   _____

Read the drama and answer the questions that follow.

A Cake for Mamsie, *continued*
Scene 2

SETTING: *The following morning, in the kitchen. Polly is using kindling to get a fire going in the old stove. Joel is following her around the kitchen, trying to be helpful. David and Phronsie are playing quietly.*

1   JOEL: It's almost eleven o'clock, Polly Pepper! You won't have it done.

POLLY: Oh, no, it isn't, Joe. It's only a quarter of nine. (*flinging wood into the stove*) The fire has to burn! And what a cake we'll have for Mamsie!

PHRONSIE: It'll be so big that Mamsie won't know what to do, will she, Polly?

POLLY: No, I don't believe she will. (*stuffing more wood into the stove*) Oh, dear! There goes the putty Ben used to mend that awful hole in the stove. It's all come out!

5   JOEL: (*going around the back of the stove to explore*) So it has. The hole is bigger than ever!

POLLY: Now, whatever shall we do? Ben's at Deacon Blodgett's!

JOEL: (*heading toward the door*) I'll run and get him. I'll bring him right home in ten minutes.

POLLY: Oh, no, you must not, Joe! It wouldn't ever be right to take Ben off from his work. Mamsie wouldn't like it.

JOEL: What will you do, then?

10   POLLY: (*getting down on her knees to look at the hole*) I'm sure I don't know. I shall have to stuff it with paper, I suppose.

JOEL: (*scornfully*) It won't stay in. Don't you know you stuffed it before, last week?

POLLY: (*sighing and sitting down on the floor*) I know.

DAVID: Can't you fix it? Then we can't have the cake. (*He flies out of the room, and then returns cradling an old leather boot-top, which he puts into Polly's hand.*) You can chip it real fine, and then it will go in.

POLLY: So we can, and you're a real good boy, Davie, to give us your treasured boot-top. That's a splendid present to help celebrate for Mamsie! (*She begins to strip the leather into little pieces.*)

15   JOEL: I'd a-given a boot-top if I had it, but I don't have anything!

POLLY: (*as she and the boys use the leather to fill up the hole in the stove*) I know you would, Joey. (*to the leather in the stove*) There now, you'll stay, I guess!

(*The door opens, and an elderly neighbor, called Grandma Bascom, walks in.*)

GRANDMA BASCOM: I hope your cake ain't in, Polly, for I've found the recipe. Also (*placing a brown parcel in the table*), there's a few raisins for you, Polly. I don't want them, and they'll make your cake go better.

POLLY: Oh! I can't thank you for the raisins and all—you're so good!

JOEL: (*whispering to David, as they examine the parcel of raisins*) They're awful hard.

Scene 3

SETTING: *Later the same morning, in the kitchen. The children, now including Ben, have gathered around the old stove.*

20 POLLY: And now, the cake's done!

(*She reaches into the stove to pull out the cake. It is black on top and collapsed in the center.*)

POLLY: (*setting the cake on the table*) Oh, no! And there's no time to redo it! (*turning angrily toward the stove*) I hope you're satisfied, you old thing! You've spoiled our Mamsie's birthday!

(*Polly sits down and begins to cry. Just then, the door opens, and Mrs. Beebe steps in. She immediately focuses on the crying Polly.*)

MRS. BEEBE: Well, I never!

DAVID: (*beginning to skip about with Phronsie*) It's Mrs. Beebe! Oh, it's Mrs. Beebe!

(*Polly immediately scrambles up to her feet and wipes away her tears.*)

MRS. BEEBE: You poor creatures, you! (*handing Polly a little bouquet*) Here, Polly, here's some posies for you, and …

25 POLLY: (*joyfully*) Oh, thank you for the flowers! Why, Mrs. Beebe, we can put them in here, can't we? The very thing! (*She sets the little bouquet in the hollow of the cake, and all five children stand back to admire it.*)

MRS. BEEBE: The very thing! It looks beautiful, I declare! And now, I must run right along, or Mr. Beebe will be worrying. (*She exits.*)

BEN: It looks good enough to eat, anyway!

POLLY: Well, we tried. Now, boys, call Mamsie; everything's ready.

(*Joel and David rush offstage and return with Mamsie, who clasps her hands in delight and surprise at the vision of the cake.*)

MAMSIE: Oh, children, thank you! (*admiring the cake from every side*) Polly, you simply couldn't have baked this cake in the old stove!

(*Mamsie cuts a piece of cake for each child, putting a flower on top of each piece. Then she and the children eat the cake, which turns out to taste much better than it looks.*)

30 JOEL: (*between bites of cake*) Why can't I ever have a birthday? I should think I might.

BEN: Why, you have, Joe. Eight of 'em!

JOEL: What a story! When did I have them? I never had a cake, did I, Polly?

MAMSIE: Not a cake birthday, Joel. You haven't got to that yet.

JOEL: When's it coming?

35 MAMSIE: (*laughing*) I don't know, but there's plenty of time ahead!

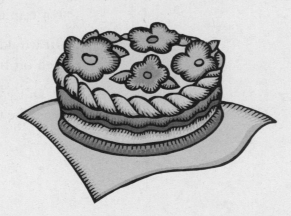

8. Based on these two scenes from the play, what characteristic do all of the Pepper children share?

    A. their helplessness

    B. their greed for sweets

    C. their love of their mother

    D. their desire for a different life

9. In Scene 3, <u>redo</u> means to do

    A. again.

    B. better.

    C. angrily.

    D. quickly.

10. From Polly's response to Mrs. Beebe's statement "Here, Polly, here's some <u>posies</u> for you," you can infer that <u>posies</u> are

    A. gifts.

    B. flowers.

    C. decorations.

    D. wishes.

11. Which quotation BEST supports the inference that the old stove often causes problems for the Pepper family?

    A. "The hole is bigger than ever!"

    B. "I'll bring him right home in ten minutes."

    C. "It wouldn't ever be right to take Ben off from his work."

    D. "Can't you fix it? Then we can't have the cake."

12. Scenes 2 and 3 build on the earlier scene from "A Cake for Mamsie" by showing how

A. Polly's efforts result in disappointment.

B. the Pepper children work out their problems.

C. poorly the children are able to make their wishes come true.

D. selfish Mamsie is for allowing celebrations of only her birthday.

13. Based on scenes 2 and 3, what can you conclude is one of the themes of this play?

A. the need for money

B. the need for surprises

C. the need for good luck

D. the need for cooperation

14. What does Mamsie mean when she says, "Not a cake birthday, Joel. You haven't got to that yet"? Use details from the passage to support your answer.

_____

_____

_____

_____

Read the story and answer the questions that follow.

Rosa and the Rose-Colored Glasses PART I

1. ON HER WAY HOME FROM SCHOOL ONE GLOOMY AFTERNOON, ROSA SEES SOMETHING UNUSUAL ON THE SIDEWALK.

WHAT ARE THESE?

HEY, HOW DO I LOOK IN THESE GLASSES?

WOW! JEFF, IF ONLY YOU COULD SEE WHAT I CAN SEE!

1. Read this entry from a thesaurus.

   rose-colored *adjective.* optimistic

   Synonyms: bright, cheerful, confident, hopeful, idealistic, positive, trusting

   Antonyms: gloomy, pessimistic

   Based on this entry, you can conclude that the glasses Rosa finds are described as <u>rose-colored</u> because

   A. they are pink.

   B. they make things look positive.

   C. they help Rosa feel more confident.

   D. their frames have bright sparkles on them.

2. What is the purpose of the picture in panel 6?

   A. It suggests that Jeff is in a bad mood.

   B. It contrasts reality with what Rosa's glasses show.

   C. It shows how the rose-colored glasses change the weather.

   D. It reveals a prediction about the future.

3. In panel 8, why does Rosa say, "I don't know what you're talking about"?

   A. She wants Jeff to stop talking.

   B. She can't hear what Jeff is telling her.

   C. She doesn't realize that she's getting wet.

   D. She doesn't understand what *soaked* means.

4. Based on her reaction to the discovery of the <u>rose-colored</u> glasses, you can infer that Rosa tends to be

   A. greedy.

   B. clumsy.

   C. confused.

   D. enthusiastic.

5. Based on his reaction to the discovery of the <u>rose-colored</u> glasses, you can infer that Jeff tends to be

    A. bossy.

    B. pessimistic.

    C. practical.

    D. argumentative.

6. What does the theme of this story MOST LIKELY have to do with?

    A. fantasy and reality

    B. the dangers of litter

    C. the changing seasons

    D. the power of optimism

7. How do the visuals in the graphic novel help you understand what is happening? Cite at least one panel in your response.

    _____

    _____

    _____

    _____

Read the story and answer the questions that follow.

Rosa and the Rose-Colored Glasses PART II

8. What does the reader learn from the pictures in panels 9 and 10?

   A. Rosa's homework has not been finished.

   B. Rosa does not usually do her homework.

   C. Rosa prefers doing reading homework over math homework.

   D. Rosa usually watches TV after finishing her homework.

9. What might be an antonym for daydream?

   A. fantasy

   B. reality

   C. adventure

   D. mystery

10. In panel 12, Rosa concludes that Jeff is jealous of her, but it is more likely that he is

    A. angry at her.

    B. making fun of her.

    C. competing with her.

    D. concerned about her.

11. In panel 16, daydreaming refers to

    A. imagining things.

    B. sleeping during the day.

    C. thinking about the weather.

    D. pretending your homework is finished.

12. Based on the events in this story, what can you predict is MOST LIKELY to happen next?

    A. Rosa will fail to do her homework again.

    B. Jeff will ask Rosa to give him the glasses.

    C. Rosa will use the glasses only sometimes for fun.

    D. Rosa's teacher will tell her parents about the glasses.

13. Which BEST states a theme of this story?

    A. It is best not to lie about your homework.

    B. It is best to avoid the rain if at all possible.

    C. It is best to share things with your friends.

    D. It is best not to lose sight of what is really happening.

14. How do the visuals in the graphic novel help you understand what is happening? Cite at least one panel in your response.

    _____

    _____

    _____

    _____

Read the story and answer the questions that follow.

How Sun, Moon, and Wind Went Out to Dinner
adapted from an Indian folktale
by Joseph Jacobs

1   It was said that Sun, Moon, and Wind were the children of a distant Star. One day, they went out to dine with their friends, Thunder and Lightning, while their mother, Star, waited alone for her children's return.

Now both Sun and Wind were greedy and selfish. They enjoyed the great feast that had been prepared for them, but they had no thought of saving any of it to take home to their mother. Gentle Moon, however, did not forget her. Of every dainty dish that was brought round, she placed a small <u>portion</u> under one of her beautiful long fingernails. She kept these treats so that Star might also have a share in the feast.

Star kept watch for her children all night long with her little bright eye. When they returned, she asked, "Well, children, what have you brought home for me?"

Then Sun, who was the eldest, said, "I have brought nothing home for you. I went out to enjoy myself with my friends. I did not go to fetch a dinner for my mother!"

5   And Wind said, "Neither have I brought anything home for you, Mother. You could hardly expect me to bring a collection of good things for you. After all, I went out only for my own pleasure."

But Moon said, "Mother, fetch a plate, see what I have brought you." And shaking her hands she showered down such a dinner as had never been seen before.

Then Star turned to Sun and spoke thus. "You went out to amuse yourself with your friends and feasted and enjoyed yourself, without any thought of your mother at home. Therefore, you shall be cursed. From now on, your rays shall ever be hot and scorching. They shall burn all that they touch. The people of Earth shall hate you and cover their heads when you appear."

And that is why the sun is so hot to this day.

Then Star turned to Wind and said, "You who also forgot your mother in the midst of your selfish pleasures—hear your doom. You shall always blow in the hot dry weather. You shall parch and shrivel all living things. The people of Earth shall detest and avoid you from this very time."

10 And that is why the wind in the hot weather is so disagreeable.

But to Moon she said, "Daughter, you remembered your mother and kept for her a share in your own enjoyment. Therefore, from now on you shall be ever cool, calm, and bright. No poisonous glare shall <u>accompany</u> your pure rays. The people of Earth shall always call you blessed."

And that is why the moon's light is so soft, cool, and beautiful, even to this day.

1. The word <u>portion</u> in paragraph 2 means

   A. part.

   B. plate.

   C. circle.

   D. snack.

2. The word <u>accompany</u> in paragraph 11 means

   A. to bless.

   B. to shine brightly.

   C. to make toxic.

   D. to go along with.

3. Unlike Moon, what do Sun and Wind seem to believe is important?

   A. their own pleasure

   B. enjoying good food

   C. taking care of others

   D. making their mother angry

4. How does the narrator seem to view Star?

   A. as too demanding

   B. as greedy and selfish

   C. as gentle and bright

   D. as supremely powerful

5. Based on this story, one could conclude that those who told this story MOST LIKELY saw the sun as

A. a giver of life.

B. a source of suffering.

C. a peacemaker.

D. an unimportant being.

6. Which was MOST LIKELY an important value in the culture from which this story comes?

A. keeping things to oneself

B. making do with what one has

C. competition between siblings

D. generosity toward one's parents

7. Explain how Moon differs from Sun and Wind. Use details from the passage to support your answer.

_____

_____

_____

_____

Read the story and answer the questions that follow.

Phaeton

adapted from a Greek myth
by Thomas Bulfinch

1   As the saying goes, pride goes before a fall. In Phaeton's case, his pride led him to fall from the greatest heights possible.

Phaeton was the son of Apollo, who rode the chariot that bore the sun across the sky every day. One day, Apollo foolishly vowed to Phaeton, "Ask what you will, the gift shall be yours." Phaeton immediately asked to drive the chariot of the sun.

Apollo shook his radiant head in warning. "I beg you to withdraw this request," he admonished. "It is not safe, nor is it suited to your youth and strength. In your <u>ignorance</u> you wish to do that which not even the gods themselves may do. None but myself may drive the flaming car of day. Not even Zeus, whose terrible right arm hurls the thunderbolts, may do so.

"The first part of the way is so steep that the horses can hardly climb it. The middle is high up in the heavens, so far above Earth and the sea that I gaze upon them with alarm. The last part of the road descends rapidly and requires most careful driving. Add to all this, the heaven is all the time turning round and carrying the stars with it. Suppose I should lend you the chariot, what would you do? Could you keep your course while the sphere was revolving under you? Indeed, the road is through the midst of frightful monsters. You pass by the horns of the Bull, in front of the Archer, near the Lion's jaws, and where the Scorpion stretches its arms in one direction and the Crab in another.

5   "Nor will you find it easy to guide those horses; their breasts are full of fire, which they breathe forth from their mouths and nostrils. I can scarcely govern them myself. Please, I beg you to choose more wisely."

But Phaeton proudly held to his demand, and Apollo, having made a vow, could not deny what Phaeton had asked. At last, he led the way to the golden chariot, while the Dawn threw open the purple doors of the east and showed the pathway strewn with roses. The stars withdrew. Apollo ordered the Hours to harness up the horses. They obeyed, led the horses forth, and attached the reins.

Apollo advised his son, "You will see the marks of the wheels. They will serve to guide you. Go not too high, or you will burn the heavenly dwellings. Go not too low, or you will set Earth on fire. The middle course is safest and best."

Phaeton sprang into the chariot, grasped the reins, and thanked his father.

The horses darted forward and soon perceived that the load they drew was lighter than usual. They rushed headlong and left the road. Terrified, Phaeton had neither the knowledge nor the power to guide them. He then looked down upon Earth and grew pale, and he wished he had never touched his father's horses.

10   Then, seeing the great Scorpion, his courage failed, and the reins fell from his hands. The horses went off into unknown regions of the sky. They hurled the chariot now up in high heaven, and then down almost to Earth. The clouds began to smoke, the mountaintops were set on fire, the fields were parched with heat, the plants withered, the trees with their leafy branches burned, and the harvest was ablaze! But these are small things. Great cities perished, with their walls and towers; whole nations with their people were consumed to ashes! Earth cracked open, and the sea shrank up. Where before was water, it became a dry plain, and the mountains that lie beneath the waves lifted up their heads and became islands.

At last, Earth looked up to heaven, and called on Zeus for his aid.

In reply, Zeus thundered. Brandishing a lightning bolt in his right hand, he launched it against Phaeton. The boy fell like a shooting star toward Earth. Eridanus, the great river, received him and cooled his burning frame.

8. According to the saying "pride goes before a fall," what happens to those who are too proud?

   A. They encounter trouble and loss.

   B. They become clumsy and have accidents.

   C. They are rewarded for their efforts.

   D. They get what they want before others do.

9. The word <u>ignorance</u> in paragraph 3 refers to a lack of

   A. desire.

   B. strength.

   C. knowledge.

   D. importance.

10. As the behavior of Apollo's horses shows, what is one main difference between Phaeton and Apollo?

    A. Phaeton is speedier.

    B. Phaeton is less powerful.

    C. Phaeton is more daring.

    D. Phaeton cares less about others.

11. How does the narrator seem to view Phaeton?

    A. with ridicule

    B. with pride

    C. with some pity

    D. with anger on his behalf

12. According to this story, which was MOST LIKELY an important Greek value?

   A. taking no risks

   B. caring for the earth

   C. keeping one's vows

   D. obeying one's parents

13. In this story, the conflict between Apollo and Phaeton represents the differences between

   A. wisdom and youth.

   B. humility and pride.

   C. strength and intelligence.

   D. faithfulness and dishonesty.

14. Why does Apollo say, "I beg you to withdraw this request"? Use details from the passage to support your response.

_____

_____

_____

_____

Read the passage and answer the questions that follow.

Anna Howard Shaw

1   Every century has its <u>pioneers</u>, the people whose ideas and accomplishments seem to be ahead of their time. In the 1800s, Anna Howard Shaw was one of those pioneers. She was one of the first women to become a Methodist minister. She also earned a medical degree. Then, she committed the last half of her life to speaking and organizing for women's rights.

Beginnings

Shaw's early life included much adventure and hardship. In 1851, when she was only four years old, she survived a near shipwreck. She, her mother, and five brothers and sisters were on their way from England to the United States, where her father was already living. Toward the beginning of the trip, their ship was caught in a three-day storm. "The first vivid memory I have is that of being on shipboard and having a mighty wave roll over me," she later wrote. Luckily, another ship rescued them and towed their leaking ship back to England. Their second attempt to cross the Atlantic was uneventful. Anna and her family settled in Massachusetts.

Then, in 1859, when she was twelve years old, another adventure began. Anna's father sent her, her mother, and five brothers and sisters to live on a frontier claim in the wilderness of northern Michigan. Their log cabin had no floor and only holes for the door and windows. The family also had no horses, few tools, and—until Anna herself dug one— no well. Through hard work and creativity, the family finished their log cabin, farmed the land, and survived.

Minister and Doctor

When she was fourteen years old, Shaw announced to her father, "Someday I am going to college." She had never heard of a woman going to college. Indeed, college seemed to her "as remote as the most distant star." Nevertheless, she later wrote, "I hitched my little wagon to that star and never afterward wholly lost sight of its friendly gleam." Her determination paid off. First, she studied at Albion College in Michigan for two years. Then, she earned a degree in theology (1878) and one in medicine (1886) from Boston University.

5   At the same time that she announced her intention to go to college, Shaw also decided to be a preacher. "For some reason I wanted to preach," she wrote, "to talk to people, to tell them things. Just why, just what, I did not yet know." In 1870, she preached her first sermon, and in 1871, she was given a preacher's license. Then, in 1880, Shaw became the first woman to be ordained in the Protestant Methodist Church.

Suffragist

From 1878 to 1885, Shaw served as the minister to two congregations on Cape Cod, Massachusetts. But in 1885, she left this ministry to preach for women's <u>rights</u>. At the time, most women could not vote in the United States. Shaw saw earning the right to vote, or suffrage, as the solution for many of the problems women faced. She later wrote, "As man's equal before the law, woman could demand her rights, asking favors from no one. With all my heart I joined in the crusade of the men and women who were fighting for her. My real work had begun."

By 1890, Shaw had become an official lecturer for the National American Woman Suffrage Association (NAWSA). Then, in 1904, she became the president of NAWSA. Some say that Shaw did not have the administrative abilities needed to be an effective leader. In fact, a rival group, the National Women's Party, split off from NAWSA in 1913. But under Shaw's leadership, the number of suffrage workers grew from 17,000 to 200,000. Also, by 1914, twelve states had granted women full suffrage.

In 1915, Shaw resigned from the presidency of NAWSA. She continued to lecture for suffrage, however. By the time she died in 1919, she had spoken for women's rights in every state of the union. In the following year, the Nineteenth Amendment to the U.S. Constitution was ratified. Women had finally won full suffrage.

1. In paragraph 1, Anna Howard Shaw is called a <u>pioneer</u> because she

   A. traveled west.

   B. did new things.

   C. lived on the frontier.

   D. had many careers.

2. Which of the following is the BEST summary of the section titled "Beginnings"?

   A. Anna Howard Shaw experienced a near shipwreck as a four-year-old child.

   B. Anna Howard Shaw enjoyed the many adventures she experienced during her journeys as a child.

   C. Anna Howard Shaw was born in England but moved to Massachusetts and then Michigan.

   D. Anna Howard Shaw survived many hardships, first in leaving England and then in moving to Michigan.

3. In paragraph 4, why did Anna Howard Shaw say that college was like a star?

   A. Going to college seemed like an unlikely thing to do.

   B. Women were not allowed to go to college until later.

   C. She thought she would need a lot of money to go to college.

   D. There were no colleges in Michigan at that time.

4. Which of the following is the BEST summary of the section titled "Suffragist"?

   A. After a career as a minister, Anna Howard Shaw became an important leader in the suffrage movement.

   B. Anna Howard Shaw was the president of the National American Woman Suffrage Association for more than ten years.

   C. While Anna Howard Shaw led the National American Woman Suffrage Association, many states granted women full suffrage.

   D. Through the hard work of women like Anna Howard Shaw, the suffrage movement was a success, and by 1920 all American women could vote.

5. As it is used in paragraph 6, <u>right</u> means

    A. something that is correct or true.

    B. an interest in or ownership of a property.

    C. a claim that is legal, just, or fair.

    D. the direction that is opposite of the left.

6. Which statement BEST describes the author's point of view on Anna Howard Shaw?

    A. Anna Howard Shaw was the greatest suffragist of her time.

    B. Anna Howard Shaw made important contributions to women's suffrage.

    C. Anna Howard Shaw was not likely a capable leader.

    D. Anna Howard Shaw was more effective as a suffragist than as a minister.

7. What is the "real work" Shaw refers to when she says, "My real work had begun"? Describe this work using details from the passage.

_____

_____

_____

_____

Read the passage and answer the questions that follow.

excerpted and adapted from

The Story of a Pioneer

by Anna Howard Shaw

In 1915, Anna Howard Shaw published her autobiography, The Story of a Pioneer. *In this selection from the book, she tells two stories about her experiences in the late 1800s. At the time, she was vice president of NAWSA. In the selection, she calls Susan B. Anthony, president of NAWSA, "Aunt Susan."*

Going Somewhere

1   It was at the time of these campaigns that I was elected Vice-President of the National Association and Lecturer at Large, and the latter office brought in its train a glittering variety of experiences. On one occasion an episode occurred which "Aunt Susan" never afterward wearied of describing. There was a wreck somewhere on the road on which I was to travel to meet a lecture engagement, and the trains going my way were not running. Looking up the track, however, I saw a train coming from the opposite direction. I at once grasped my hand-luggage and started for it.

"Wait! Wait!" cried Miss Anthony. "That train's going the wrong way!"

"At least it's going SOMEWHERE!" I replied, tersely, as the train stopped, and I climbed the steps.

Looking back when the train had started again, I saw "Aunt Susan" standing in the same spot on the platform and staring after it with incredulous eyes; but I was right, for I discovered that by going up into another state I could get a train which would take me to my destination in time for the lecture that night. It was a fine illustration of my pet theory that if one intends to get somewhere it is better to start, even in the wrong direction, than to stand still.

A Lack of Understanding

5   Again and again in our work we had occasion to marvel over men's lack of understanding of the <u>views</u> of women, even of those nearest and dearest to them; and we had an especially striking illustration of this at one of our hearings in Washington. A certain distinguished gentleman (we will call him Mr. H——) was chairman of the Judiciary, and after we had said what we wished to say, he remarked:

"Your arguments are logical. Your cause is just. The trouble is that women don't want suffrage. My wife doesn't want it. I don't know a single woman who does want it."

As it happened for this unfortunate gentleman, his wife was present at the hearing and sitting beside Miss Anthony. She listened to his words with surprise, and then whispered to "Aunt Susan":

"How CAN he say that? I want suffrage, and I've told him so a hundred times in the last twenty years."

"Tell him again NOW," urged Miss Anthony. "Here's your chance to impress it on his memory."

10   "Here!" gasped the wife. "Oh, I wouldn't dare."

"Then may I tell him?"

"Why—yes! He can think what he pleases, but he has no right to publicly misrepresent me."

The assent, hesitatingly begun, finished on a sudden note of firmness. Miss Anthony stood up.

"It may interest Mr. H——," she said, "to know that his wife DOES wish to vote, and that for twenty years she has wished to vote, and has often told him so, though he has evidently forgotten it. She is here beside me and has just made this explanation."

15   Mr. H—— stammered and hesitated, and finally decided to laugh. But there was no mirth in the sound he made, and I am afraid his wife had a bad quarter of an hour when they met a little later in the privacy of their home.

8. What point of view does Anna Howard Shaw express in the section titled "Going Somewhere"?

    A. It is foolish to go the wrong way.

    B. Going anywhere is better than staying put.

    C. You never know what the future holds.

    D. It is important to have goals.

9. Which of the following is the BEST summary of the section titled "A Lack of Understanding"?

    A. A congressman does not understand his own wife.

    B. A congressman tries to argue against women's suffrage.

    C. A congressman and his wife disagree about women's suffrage.

    D. A congressman is corrected in his belief that women do not want suffrage.

10. As it is used in paragraph 5, <u>views</u> means

    A. visions.

    B. opinions.

    C. landscapes.

    D. pictures.

Use "Anna Howard Shaw" and the excerpt from *The Story of a Pioneer* to answer questions 11–14.

11. What aspect of Anna Howard Shaw's character can be seen in the excerpt from her autobiography, *The Story of a Pioneer,* that is not discussed in the biography, "Anna Howard Shaw"?

    A. her sense of humor

    B. her determination

    C. her willingness to work hard

    D. her creativity in solving problems

12. Which part of Anna Howard Shaw's life does the excerpt from *The Story of a Pioneer* tell about?

A. just before she decided to leave the ministry

B. after she gave up her ministry but before her NAWSA presidency

C. during her NAWSA presidency

D. after she resigned from her NAWSA presidency

13. Which fact from "Anna Howard Shaw" could BEST be used to disprove the congressman's statement in *The Story of a Pioneer* that "women don't want suffrage"?

A. Anna Howard Shaw thought women's suffrage would solve many problems.

B. A rival group split off from NAWSA in 1913.

C. In the early 1900s, the number of suffrage workers grew into the hundreds of thousands.

D. Anna Howard Shaw continued to lecture for women's suffrage even after giving up her leadership position.

14. Explain why a secondary source about Shaw might be a more reliable source than a primary source written by Shaw. Use details from the passages to support your ideas.

_____

_____

_____

_____

Read the passage and answer the questions that follow.

The Columbian Exchange

1   After Christopher Columbus landed in the Caribbean in 1492, plants, animals, and, unfortunately, diseases, began to cross the Atlantic Ocean. Some were brought from Europe to the Americas, and others were brought back from the Americas to Europe. Historians now call this movement of plants, animals, and diseases the Columbian Exchange. It changed everyday life in both Europe and the Americas. For example, people began to eat new foods—including many that you probably eat regularly today. The following are some of the items and animals involved in this great exchange.

From the New World to the Old

Potatoes

Potatoes have been cultivated in the Andes Mountains of South America for nearly two thousand years. By the end of the 1500s, the Spanish and Italians were growing potatoes, too. The potato soon became an important part of the cuisines of Germany, Poland, Russia, Britain, and Ireland. Today, only grains are cultivated more widely than potatoes, which are grown in at least eighty different countries throughout the world.

Tomatoes

Like potatoes, tomatoes are members of the nightshade family that are native to South America. (Pepper, eggplant, and tobacco plants are also members of the nightshade family.) The Inca and the Aztec both cultivated tomatoes. Unlike potatoes, tomatoes were not immediately popular with Europeans. In fact, their fruit was thought to be poisonous! However, the Spanish and Italians began to use tomatoes in their cuisine. Today, of course, tomatoes are especially associated with Italian cooking.

Chocolate

The scientific name of the cacao tree is *Cacao theobroma,* which means "food of the gods." The heavenly food made from the beans of the cacao tree is chocolate. The Aztec cultivated cacao beans. They made a bitter drink called *xocoatl* from the beans. The Spanish conqueror Hernando Cortes called this drink <u>divine</u>. He sent three chests of the beans to Spain. In Europe, the drink was sweetened and flavored with cinnamon and vanilla. Then, in the 1800s, Europeans began to make chocolate that could be eaten instead of drunk. In 1876, milk chocolate was first made in Switzerland. Today, the Swiss are the world's leading consumers of chocolate, with as much as twenty-two pounds of chocolate eaten per person every year.

From the Old World to the New

Horses

5   The fossil record shows that the horse evolved mostly in North America. About two million years ago, animals belonging to the genus *Equus* (which includes the horse) had spread to South America, Europe, Asia, and Africa. However, for unknown reasons, the horse disappeared from the Americas about ten thousand to eight thousand years ago. Spanish explorers returned the horse to its native home in the 1500s.

Apples

European settlers brought apples with them to North America. At the time, apples were not eaten raw. They were mostly used to make cider, or apple juice. As settlers moved westward, they brought apples with them, often planting the trees near their homes. Today, five-and-a-half million tons of apples are produced in the United States every year.

Sugarcane

Sugarcane did not originally come from Europe. It came from the faraway island of New Guinea, just north of Australia. From there, sugarcane spread throughout the South Pacific and to India. Then, from India its cultivation spread westward to Persia and then throughout the Mediterranean world. On his second trip to the New World, Columbus brought along sugarcane from the Canary Islands. Its production soon became important to the economies of the West Indies, Brazil, Mexico, and later the southern United States.

    The process of globalization started long before 1492 and continues to the <u>present</u>. However, the Columbian Exchange stands out for its thorough transformation of the cultures and ecology of so much of the world.

1. Why is the movement of plants, animals, and diseases described in this passage MOST LIKELY called the Columbian Exchange?

   A. Columbus described the exchange in his writings.

   B. The exchange began with the arrival of Columbus in the Caribbean.

   C. Columbus was responsible for organizing the exchange.

   D. The exchange was begun to honor the achievements of Columbus.

2. Which of the following details from the passage BEST supports the idea that the Columbian Exchange changed everyday life in Europe?

   A. "The potato soon became an important part of the cuisines of Germany, Poland, Russia, Britain, and Ireland."

   B. "Then, in the 1800s, Europeans began to make chocolate that could be eaten instead of drunk."

   C. "At the time, apples were not eaten raw. They were mostly used to make cider, or apple juice."

   D. "On his second trip to the New World, Columbus brought along sugarcane from the Canary Islands."

3. Which BEST compares the text structure of the paragraph titled "Tomatoes" with that of the other paragraphs of this passage?

   A. "Tomatoes" compares and contrasts ideas, whereas the text structure of the other sections is mostly cause and effect.

   B. "Tomatoes" tells about problems and solutions, whereas the text structure of the other sections is mostly chronological order.

   C. "Tomatoes" compares and contrasts ideas, whereas the text structure of the other sections is mostly chronological order.

   D. "Tomatoes" tells about problems and solutions, whereas the text structure of the other sections is mostly cause and effect.

4. From the context in paragraph 4, you can conclude that the word <u>divine</u> has to do with

   A. gods.

   B. chocolate.

   C. conquering.

   D. drinking.

5. Read this sentence from the passage.

> **About two million years ago, animals in the genus *Equus* (which includes the horse) had spread to South America, Europe, Asia, and Africa.**

Based on this statement, you can infer that

A. the Columbian Exchange was unusual in that it included plants as well as animals.

B. the Columbian Exchange was most likely much less important than historians believe.

C. the Columbian Exchange was not the only example of the global movement of species.

D. the Columbian Exchange resulted in the return of many plants and animals to their native homes.

6. As it is used in paragraph 8, the word <u>present</u> refers to

A. a gift.

B. the current time.

C. displaying something.

D. being in a nearby location.

7. Based on the details in this passage, what does the term <u>globalization</u> mean?

_____

_____

_____

_____

Read the passage and answer the questions that follow.

Three Child Kings

1   To be president of the United States, a person must be at least thirty-five years old. In a monarchy, on the other hand, there is usually no minimum age requirement. Throughout history, children have been crowned the kings and queens of nations.

Tutankhamen

Tutankhamen, also known as King Tut, is the most famous of all the ancient Egyptian pharaohs. He did not earn this fame by doing great things, however. He is famous for his tomb, which was discovered in 1922. It held hundreds of treasures, from which we have learned much about the lives of ancient Egyptians.

Born in 1343 BCE, Tutankhamen became king when he was about nine years old. Government officials helped the young king rule.

Tutankhamen not only became pharaoh when he was young but he also died young, when he was only eighteen. He was buried west of the Nile, in the Valley of the Kings, where many other pharaohs were also buried.

The Sun King

5   King Louis XIV of France once said, "I am the <u>state</u>." He described himself this way because during his long rule, he took on far more power than any other French king had done before.

Louis became king in 1643, when he was four years old. The early years of his rule are known as the Regency. A regent is a person who rules in the place of a monarch who is too young or otherwise unable to rule a nation or people. Until Louis came of age in 1652, he had two regents. They were Queen Anne of Austria, his mother, and Cardinal Jules Mazarin, the chief minister of France.

In 1648, a civil war broke out in France. The Parliament of Paris, which was the supreme law court in France, and the nobility both objected to the growing power of the royal government. During the war, Louis, Queen Anne, and Cardinal Mazarin fled from Paris. Louis did not return to Paris until October 1652.

This war had a strong influence on Louis and his ideas about government. After the death of Cardinal Mazarin in 1661, Louis claimed all of the power of the state for himself. Although he would appoint ministers as advisers, he declared that he alone would make all decisions of government. Louis XIV ruled in this way for fifty-five years.

The Last Emperor of China

Like Tutankhamen, the Xuantong emperor of China, better known as Puyi, ruled only a short time. However, Puyi's reign did not end with his death. It ended with a revolution.

10   Puyi became emperor when his uncle died in November 1908. Puyi was only three years old. He ruled, with his father as regent, for hardly more than three years. Revolution had been brewing in China since 1900, before Puyi was born, and on October 10, 1911, the revolution succeeded. Puyi abdicated, or gave up the throne, in February 1912.

For much of the rest of his life, Puyi continued to live in Beijing. From 1934 to 1945, however, he ruled over a Japanese state in Manchuria, a province in northeastern China. Because he worked with the Japanese when they were at war with China, he was later imprisoned as a war criminal. <u>Pardoned</u> in 1959, he worked in a botanical garden and later as a researcher. He died in 1967.

8. Which BEST describes the main idea of this passage?

   A. Children have sometimes been the rulers of nations.

   B. Child monarchs tend to suffer an early death or are forced to abdicate.

   C. Child monarchs need the help of a regent in order to rule.

   D. Children do not have the skills to be a monarch.

9. Which quotation shows why Tutankhamen MOST LIKELY did not rule for very long?

   A. His tomb "held hundreds of treasures."

   B. "Born in 1343 BCE, Tutankhamen became king when he was about nine years old."

   C. Tutankhamen "died young, when he was only eighteen."

   D. "He was buried west of the Nile, in the Valley of the Kings."

10. As it is used in paragraph 5, the word <u>state</u> refers to

   A. saying something.

   B. being a certain way.

   C. a nation or government.

   D. one of the fifty United States.

11. Read this sentence from the passage.

> **This war had a strong influence on Louis and his ideas about government.**

Based on the details in paragraph 8, how did the civil war affect Louis?

A. He allowed the states to govern themselves.

B. He believed the king should have a lot of power.

C. He became unable to make decisions himself.

D. He decided that Cardinal Mazarin should be king.

12. From the context in paragraph 11, you can conclude that the word <u>pardoned</u> means

A. hired.

B. jailed.

C. forgiven.

D. punished.

13. Which BEST describes the text structure of each of the sections of this passage?

A. cause and effect

B. problem and solution

C. compare and contrast

D. chronological order

14. What do each of the kings described in the passage have in common? Why is this unique?

_____

_____

_____

_____

Read the passage and answer the questions that follow.

Making Honey

1   People have enjoyed honey since the Ice Age, when they used the smoke from torches to calm bees and steal their honey. For centuries, honey was the main source of sugar for most people. By the 1600s, people had begun to develop ways to keep bees for their honey and for help pollinating plants. During that century, honeybees were also brought to North America for the first time. Today, millions of pounds of honey are produced in the United States every year.

How Bees Make Honey

Honeybees live together in hives or nests. Each type of honeybee has a job. The queen bee lays eggs—as many as one thousand every day. The drones mate with the queen. And the workers take care of all of the tasks that keep the hive going, including making honey.

Bees make honey from nectar. Nectar is a sweet, watery fluid that flowers make. The worker bees, known as field bees, gather nectar from flowers in as many as ten trips every day. A field bee sucks up the nectar from a flower through its straw-shaped proboscis into its second stomach, called the honey stomach. In each nectar-gathering trip, a honeybee may visit dozens of flowers. When its honey stomach is full, the field bee returns to the hive.

In the hive, field bees pass the nectar to the worker bees known as house bees. The house bees "chew" on the nectar, mixing it with <u>enzymes</u>. Some of these enzymes break down the nectar's complex sugar, called sucrose, changing it into simpler sugars, called glucose and fructose. These simpler sugars are easier for bees to digest. Other enzymes change some of the glucose to acid and hydrogen peroxide. The acidity kills any bacteria that might get into the honey.

5   The house bees then place the still-watery honey into beeswax cells. They fan the cells with their wings, so that the water in the honey will evaporate more quickly. When the honey is finished being made, the bees cap the honey cell with beeswax.

How Humans Process Honey

The honey you buy at a grocery store or farmers market does not go straight from the beehive into a jar. The beekeeper takes several steps to prepare honey for the market.

First, the beekeeper needs to remove the honey from the honeycomb. The honeycomb is the structure of beeswax cells that hold the honey. The beekeeper scrapes the wax caps off of the combs. Then, the beekeeper uses a machine called an extractor to get the honey out of the combs. The extractor spins the combs so that the honey is forced to the sides of the machine. The honey then falls to the bottom of the extractor, where it can be collected.

Next, the beekeeper needs to purify the honey. The beekeeper strains and filters the honey to remove bits of wax, air bubbles, pollen, and other particles. Finally, the honey may be heat-treated to prevent it from crystallizing and fermenting.

According to the National Honey Board, more than three hundred different kinds of honey are made in the United States. Each kind is made from the nectar of different flowers, including clover (the most common), alfalfa, blueberry, eucalyptus, and tupelo. Each has its own unique flavor. <u>However</u>, whatever the flavor, one amazing fact is true. The nectar of more than two million flowers may go into the production of just one pound of honey!

1. In paragraph 3, how is a honeybee's honey stomach similar to a human stomach?

   A. It receives food.

   B. It digests food.

   C. It turns nectar into food.

   D. It is used to store food.

2. The <u>enzymes</u> in paragraph 4 are MOST LIKELY a kind of

   A. bee.

   B. sugar.

   C. teeth.

   D. chemical.

3. The first two paragraphs of the section titled "How Bees Make Honey" tell about events in the order in which they happen. Which organizational pattern do the second two paragraphs use?

   A. cause and effect

   B. main idea and details

   C. problem and solution

   D. compare and contrast

4. According to the passage, field bees collect nectar, whereas house bees

   A. store nectar.

   B. make honey.

   C. collect honey.

   D. eat nectar.

5. According to the passage, how do the ways bees and humans process honey compare?

    A. Humans purify the honey, whereas bees make it.

    B. Humans use machines to make honey, whereas bees use nectar.

    C. Humans do not ferment the honey, whereas bees do.

    D. Humans use honeycombs to store honey, whereas bees use hives.

6. The use of the word <u>however</u> in paragraph 9 signals that the idea that follows will give a

    A. cause.

    B. solution.

    C. similarity.

    D. contrast.

7. Explain the process that beekeepers use to process honey.

_____

_____

_____

_____

Read the passage and answer the questions that follow.

The Steam Engine

1   The inventions we use every day are typically made in response to a problem. However, with the solution to the problem, other problems often arise. Over time, inventions change or are replaced by new inventions. The hope is that the newer inventions will solve the same problem as the older inventions without making new problems. For an example, let's look at the steam engine.

Newcomen's Engine

Very deep mines can easily get filled with water. In the 1600s, English mine owners used pumps to keep their mines dry. Horses kept the pumps going. They were attached to a wheel that ran the pump, and they turned the wheel by walking in circles. This <u>method</u> worked, but it was expensive. Mine owners had to take on the cost of feeding and caring for the horses.

An English blacksmith named Thomas Newcomen believed there should be a better way to drain mines. In 1698, another Englishman, named Thomas Savery, had patented a machine that used the suction created by condensing steam to power a pump. (When steam condenses, it becomes water again.) Newcomen also wanted to use steam as a source of power. Steam is a good source of power because water <u>expands</u> when it turns into steam. The energy of the expanding steam can be used to do work.

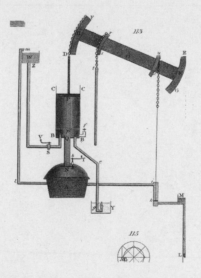

This diagram shows how the piston and cylinder work together in Newcomen's steam engine.

In 1712, Newcomen built an engine that used steam instead of horses. Like Savery's engine, Newcomen's engine used condensing steam. Unlike Savery's engine, however, Newcomen's engine also used a piston. The piston was inside a cylinder. The vacuum created by condensing steam at the bottom of the cylinder caused the piston to move down within the cylinder. Then more steam was let into the cylinder, pushing the piston back up again. In this way, the piston moved up and down and ran the pump, to which it was connected.

5   For years, the Newcomen engine was used to drain mines, as well as for other purposes.

Watt's Engine

Using Newcomen's engine was obviously better than using horses to drain mines. But his engine was far from perfect because it wasted heat.

A Scottish inventor named James Watt produced a better steam engine. He became known as the father of the modern steam engine. First, in 1765, he created an engine in which the steam condensed outside the cylinder. This engine did not waste as much heat. Then, in 1782, he made an engine that produced power when the piston moved in both directions. This engine was even more effective.

Uses of the Steam Engine

Later, other inventors improved on Watt's design. They made more powerful high-pressure engines. <u>Moreover</u>, they made engines that used several cylinders instead of just one.

By this time, steam engines were being used for much more than just pumping water out of mines. They were being used in factories, for example. In 1769, a Frenchman named Nicholas-Joseph Cugnot created a carriage that used a steam engine rather than horses as its source of power. This carriage could be considered the first automobile, but it was not practical. Other attempts to use steam engines for transportation were more successful. By 1807, an American named Robert Fulton had created a passenger steamboat. Then, in 1829, George Stephenson developed the first commercially successful train that was powered by steam.

Return of the Steam Engine?

10   In the twentieth century, the internal-combustion engine replaced the steam engine as the source of power for most vehicles. However, internal-combustion engines rely on the burning of fossil fuels, resulting in pollution and climate change. The steam engine just might offer a solution to this new problem!

8. How could the organizational pattern of the sections titled "Newcomen's Engine" and "Watt's Engine" BEST be described?

   A. Descriptions of problems follow descriptions of solutions.

   B. Descriptions of solutions follow descriptions of problems.

   C. Descriptions of solutions are included without descriptions of problems.

   D. Descriptions of problems and solutions are all jumbled together.

9. The word method in paragraph 2 refers to

   A. a costly solution.

   B. a type of machine.

   C. a job done by animals.

   D. a way of doing something.

10. In paragraph 3, what happens when water expands?

   A. It goes away.

   B. It gets bigger.

   C. It turns into liquid.

   D. It loses energy.

11. According to the passage, how did the engine that Watt built in 1782 compare with Newcomen's engine?

   A. It was more effective.

   B. It used more cylinders.

   C. It used a piston instead of steam.

   D. It wasted even more heat.

12. The use of the word <u>moreover</u> in paragraph 8 signals that the idea that follows will

    A. add to the idea that comes before it.

    B. describe a problem with the idea that comes before it.

    C. give a contrast with the idea that comes before it.

    D. tell a cause of the idea that comes before it.

13. Based on the section titled "Return of the Steam Engine?" you can conclude that steam engines

    A. create much more pollution than internal-combustion engines do.

    B. are not a good source of power for vehicles, unlike internal-combustion engines.

    C. rely on the burning of fossil fuels less than internal-combustion engines do.

    D. are almost certainly going to replace internal-combustion engines in the future.

14. What inspired Newcomen to build his steam engine? Use details from the passage to support your answer.

_____

_____

_____

_____

Read the passage and answer the questions that follow.

The Forest Biomes

1   A biome is a community of plants, animals, and other organisms. There are six major types of biomes: forest, freshwater, marine, desert, grassland, and tundra. Of these, the forest biomes are among the most varied. Covering about one-third of the land area on Earth, forests occur in both the tropics and subarctic regions, as well as at all latitudes in between. There are three types of forest biomes.

Tropical Forest

Tropical forests grow near the equator. They are characterized by their great diversity of species and their steady climate. There is no winter, and both the temperature and the hours of daylight vary little throughout the year. Rainfall typically averages between 80 and 200 inches per year.

Lush vegetation thrives in these damp forests. Where rainfall is evenly distributed throughout the year, the trees are mostly evergreen, which means they keep their leaves year-round. The tallest trees are 75 to 100 feet tall, and their leaves form the uppermost layer of a thick, many-layered canopy. In a tropical forest, little light reaches the ground, and most animals live in the trees.

Temperate Forest

Temperate forests grow in regions of North America, Europe, China, and Australia that see distinct seasons every year. The climate in these regions is much more variable and much less wet than that of a tropical forest. For example, the number of daylight hours varies throughout the year. Temperatures also vary, often falling below freezing in the winter. Rainfall typically averages about 40 inches per year.

Lesson
Quizzes

5   The canopy of a temperate forest is not as thick as that of a tropical forest. Some light reaches the ground. Therefore, many different plants can grow at the lower levels of a temperate forest. These plants include shrubs, ferns, flowers, and mosses. Also, unlike in tropical forests, in temperate forests animals live on or near the ground as well as in the trees. In addition to insects, lizards, snakes, and birds, mammals as small as foxes and rabbits and as large as black bears live in temperate forests.

There are two types of temperate forests: <u>deciduous</u> and evergreen. In a deciduous forest, most trees lose their leaves in the autumn and grow new ones in the spring. Evergreen temperate forests are found where the winters are milder. These include the humid, misty forests of the northern Pacific coast of North America, where the redwoods, the largest trees in the world, grow.

Boreal Forest

Boreal forests grow in northernmost North America, Europe, and Asia. The climate in these regions is much <u>harsher</u> than it is in tropical and temperate forests. Winters are long, cold, and dark. Summers are short and cool, allowing a growing season of only about one-hundred-thirty days. Precipitation falls mostly as snow.

Coniferous trees, such as pine, spruce, hemlock, and fir trees, grow in boreal forests. These are evergreen trees with needle-like leaves that hold water during the dry winter. Like tropical forests, boreal forests have a thick canopy that allows little light to reach the ground. Therefore, as in tropical forests, undergrowth is limited.

In spite of the harsh climate, many different animals make boreal forests their home. These include hawks and migratory birds, large mammals such as bears, moose, elk, and deer, and smaller mammals such as foxes, hares, chipmunks, and bats.

The Forest Biomes in Numbers

	Latitudes Equator is 0°	Temperatures	Yearly Rainfall
Tropical	23.5°S to 23.5°N	average 20°C to 25°C (68°F to 77°F)	200 cm (about 80 inches) or more
Temperate	23.5° to 50°S and 23.5° to 50°N	range from −30°C to 30°C (−22°F to 86°F)	75–150 cm (about 30–60 inches)
Boreal	50° to 60°N	very low	40–100 cm (about 20–40 inches)

1. According to the information in this passage, the three types of forest biomes are categorized based on their

   A. ages.

   B. heights.

   C. climates.

   D. continents.

2. According to the information in this passage, what determines whether or not a forest has a lot of undergrowth?

   A. the types of trees that grow in the forest

   B. the amount of rainfall the forest receives

   C. the amount of light that reaches the ground

   D. the types of animals that live in the forest

3. Read this entry from a dictionary.

   de•cid•u•ous (di-'si-ju-wəs)
   adjective. losing its leaves every year

   Which best describes the pronunciation of <u>deciduous</u> in paragraph 6?

   A. accent on the first syllable; last syllable rhymes with *fuss*

   B. accent on the first syllable; last syllable rhymes with *house*

   C. accent on the second syllable; last syllable rhymes with *fuss*

   D. accent on the second syllable; last syllable rhymes with *house*

4. The word <u>harsher</u> in paragraph 7 means

   A. colder, darker.

   B. briefer, more limited.

   C. more distant, remote.

   D. more difficult, severe.

5. Read this sentence.

   In forests, trees and other woody plants prevail.

   In which section of the passage would this sentence MOST LIKELY belong?

   A. the introductory paragraph

   B. the section titled "Tropical Forest"

   C. the section titled "Temperate Forest"

   D. the section titled "Boreal Forest"

6. Which of the following conclusions can you draw from the chart?

   A. Boreal forests do not grow south of the equator.

   B. Temperate forests are generally hotter than tropical forests.

   C. There are more temperate forests than other kinds of forests.

   D. The trees in boreal forests do not get enough rain to grow very tall.

7. How do evergreen trees thrive in boreal forests? Use details from the passage to support your answer.

   _____

   _____

   _____

   _____

Read the passage and answer the questions that follow.

Cool Cats

1   When you think of big cats, you might picture a tiger lurking in the lush tropical forests of Asia. Or, you might imagine a leopard prowling the wide grasslands of Africa. It is unlikely that you imagine either of these great creatures tracking its prey through snow. However, subspecies of both of these cats do in fact live in the boreal forests of the far north.

The Amur Tiger

The Amur tiger is also commonly known as the Siberian tiger. It lives in southeastern Russia and northern China, the region surrounding the Amur River, which forms part of the border between Russia and China. The tigers' <u>current</u> territory is much smaller than its historical territory.

Of all the subspecies of tigers, the Amur tiger is the largest—which also makes it the largest cat in the world. It can grow as long as 13 feet and weigh as much as 660 pounds.

Like other tigers—and most other big cats—Amur tigers mostly live alone. They hunt very large animals, such as elk, boar, and deer. They typically avoid humans. Females give birth to two to six cubs at a time, which they raise mostly on their own. When they are eighteen months old, the cubs begin to learn to hunt. They leave their mothers for their own territory when they are two or three years old.

The Amur Leopard

5   Like the Amur tiger, the Amur leopard once claimed a much larger region as its home. This region included Manchuria in China, the Korean Peninsula, and southeastern Russia. Now, the <u>fittest</u> population of Amur leopards occupies a much smaller area, between the Chinese border and Vladivostok in Russia.

Amur leopards also live mostly alone, except during the two or so years when cubs and their mothers live together. They hunt deer and small mammals, such as hares and rodents. These leopards have adapted well to their colder climate. In the winter, they grow a thick coat of fur, with hairs that are nearly three times the length of the hairs in their summer coat. Also, their legs are longer than those of other leopards. It is thought that these longer legs help them walk through snow.

In Danger

Like other big cats, the Amur tiger and Amur leopard are both in danger of extinction. However, even though both live in the same region of the world, the situations of these two animals are very different.

In the 1940s, only about forty Amur tigers were left in the wild. People hunted the tigers for their parts, which were used in traditional medicine. Their prey, such as boar and deer, and their habitat were also in danger from humans. However, the Soviet government decided to save the Amur tigers. They were given full protection from poaching, or illegal hunting. By the late 1980s, the Amur tiger population had grown to about five hundred. With the collapse of the Soviet Union, poaching increased. Nevertheless, the Amur tiger population now numbers about four hundred fifty. It is the healthiest tiger population in the world.

The Amur leopard, on the other hand, remains in serious danger. Only about thirty of these leopards still live in the wild. The dangers to these cats are similar to those that endanger the Amur tiger: poaching, including poaching of their prey, and the destruction of their habitat. Efforts to save the Amur leopard include both the enforcement of laws against poaching and protection of their habitat. Fortunately, in 2012 the Russian government created the 650,000-acre Land of the Leopard National Park. With this new protected area for Amur leopards, perhaps theirs, like that of the Amur tiger, will be a success story.

8. The word <u>current</u> in paragraph 2 refers to

   A. a region of land.

   B. the present time.

   C. the flow of a river.

   D. the habitat of an animal.

9. Read this entry from a dictionary.

   fit (fit) *adjective.***1**: appropriate; **2**: qualified; **3**: in good physical condition or health; **4**: (of a population) adapted, able to reproduce and grow

   Which definition BEST explains the meaning of <u>fittest</u> in paragraph 5?

   A. definition 1

   B. definition 2

   C. definition 3

   D. definition 4

10. In the section titled "In Danger," what do the stories of both the Amur tiger and the Amur leopard show?

    A. their need to find a different habitat

    B. the indifference of most humans to their survival

    C. the almost certain likelihood of their extinction

    D. the role of governments in helping species

11. Read this sentence.

    People hunt Amur leopards not to use their parts in medicine, but for their beautiful coats.

    In which section of the passage would this sentence MOST LIKELY belong?

    A. the introductory paragraph

    B. the section titled "The Amur Tiger"

    C. the section titled "The Amur Leopard"

    D. the section titled "In Danger"

Use "The Forest Biomes" and "Cool Cats" to answer questions 12–14.

12. What additional information can you conclude about boreal forests based on "Cool Cats"?

    A. They are getting warmer.

    B. Most of their species are fragile.

    C. Much of their wildlife is in danger.

    D. They are now found only near the Amur River.

13. Based on the information in "The Forest Biomes," in addition to cold and snow, to what conditions did Amur tigers need to adapt?

    A. long winter nights

    B. the necessity of migrating

    C. great variations in temperature

    D. the lack of leaves to provide shelter in winter

14. What can you learn about an animal you do not know much about based on which biome it lives in?

    _____

    _____

    _____

    _____

Read the passage and answer the questions that follow.

Yes to the Auditorium!

The citizens of the town of Westville will be voting on whether or not to approve the school budget. The budget includes money to build an auditorium at Grace Hill Middle School, which does not have an auditorium. Some people do not like this plan. The editor of the local newspaper has published letters both for and against the plan to build an auditorium. The following letter is in favor of the auditorium.

Dear Editor:

1   We are writing to you about next week's vote on the school <u>budget</u>. We would like to urge everyone to vote yes to pass the budget. Voting yes for the budget means saying yes to an auditorium for Grace Hill Middle School. Our school needs this auditorium. In fact, our entire community could benefit from this auditorium.

As you probably know, the arts are alive and well at Grace Hill Middle School. We have a thriving visual arts program with four teachers, one for every grade in the school. More than one hundred students play an instrument and <u>participate</u> in the band, orchestra, or both. Another hundred students take part in the choral program, which feeds directly into our award-winning high school choral program. Additionally, a growing number of students are petitioning the administration to help them form an after-school theater club. It is astonishing to realize how poorly the physical structure of our school supports these efforts of our students. The building provides walls for the students' artwork—and that is all. Our band, orchestra, chorus, and a cappella groups have no auditorium in which they can perform for the school.

Also, those students who play an instrument or sing are not the only ones who would benefit from the proposed auditorium. Indeed, the entire student body of Grace Hill Middle School would benefit. At present, we have no place where we can comfortably assemble. True, as many have pointed out, we do have a gym. But the gym was built for athletic events. It is not a good place in which to perform or listen to music, put on a talent show, gather to watch a film, or host a debate.

Furthermore, our middle school students and their teachers and families would not be the only members of our community to use the auditorium. After all, the auditorium at Westville High School is just about fully booked through most of the year. Therefore, Westville has been unable to host many events that the town would enjoy, such as recitals, plays, and other traveling shows. Of course, Westville does have another theater, in Jefferson Memorial Hall. However, that theater is not suitable for many events. The stage is small, and the seating is enough for only about two hundred people.

5   Finally, we should remember that Grace Hill, for whom our middle school is named, was not only the school's first principal but also a patron of the arts. She loved choral music and was one of the founders of Choir Fest, still held in Westville every spring. Moreover, she did not see the arts as a "frill," as some who oppose the auditorium describe the arts. She once wrote, "Cooperation, discipline, history, and mathematics: these are what the arts have to teach our children. But, even more important, they are an essential part of our humanity. Through the arts, we <u>appreciate</u> beauty and express who we truly are." It does not seem right that the school that bears her name should not have a space for the music and theater that she so dearly loved.

Again, please vote yes next Tuesday. The entire community will thank you.

Sincerely,

Elena Mendoza

Kathleen Ferguson

Bob Kingsley

Teachers, Grace Hill Middle School

1. Which is MOST LIKELY a reason why the authors of this letter may be biased in favor of the auditorium?

   A. They are members of the community who would like to see more shows.

   B. They are teachers at the school who would benefit most from the auditorium.

   C. They are musicians who are looking for more opportunities to perform.

   D. They are citizens of Westville who pay the taxes that will fund the auditorium.

2. Which is MOST LIKELY the reason why the authors write that "the arts are alive and well at Grace Hill Middle School"?

   A. to show that the school will certainly use an auditorium

   B. to show how well the school is doing without an auditorium

   C. to show that students are more interested in the arts than in sports

   D. to show how a lack of an auditorium is threatening the school

3. The word <u>participate</u> in paragraph 2 means

   A. to take part.

   B. to have fun.

   C. to make music.

   D. to listen carefully.

4. For what reason do the authors MOST LIKELY describe the theater at Jefferson Memorial Hall?

   A. The new auditorium will have a similar design.

   B. The theater does not meet the needs of the community.

   C. Interest in the theater shows that the community wants another one.

   D. The new auditorium will need to compete with the theater.

5. What does the word <u>budget</u> in paragraph 1 mean?

    A. a rule that says money can be spent only on a certain thing

    B. the taxes and fees that go to a board or government

    C. a plan for how money should be spent

    D. the reason why there is never enough money

6. The word <u>appreciate</u> in paragraph 5 means

    A. to grow.

    B. to study.

    C. to create.

    D. to enjoy.

7. What are the authors mostly arguing for? Be specific and include details from the letter in your answer.

_____

_____

_____

_____

Read the passage and answer the questions that follow.

No to the Auditorium!

The following letter is against the plan to build an auditorium at Grace Hill Middle School.

Dear Editor:

1   I write to encourage everyone to think hard and clearly about the future of Westville. Although I can appreciate why some will disagree with me, I firmly believe that this town does not need another auditorium. What is more, I believe that the plan to build an auditorium at Grace Hill Middle School is poorly thought out. It does not make sense for the long-term health of our community and its finances.

Before I explain my objections to the auditorium, however, I want to make one thing clear. Like many of those who support the auditorium, I am a lover of the arts. My wife and I are both members of the Westville Community Chorus. We are longtime season ticket holders for the Philharmonic Orchestra. Both of our children attended public schools, and both of our children learned to play instruments in the public schools. Our younger son, now twenty years old, still plays the trombone. Throughout his time in high school and now college, he has played with a number of different jazz bands. I certainly do not look upon the arts as a "frill." No, I believe that the arts are a necessary part of life, and a necessary part of a child's education.

Nevertheless, I do not believe that the planned auditorium is necessary for the arts education of our children. The greater part of their arts education occurs in much smaller settings, such as the classroom. Meanwhile, for performances by the band, orchestra, and chorus, the auditorium at Westville High School is more than suitable. As it is, the auditorium at the high school is empty most of the time. Instead of building another auditorium that will also be empty most of the time, why not get as much use as we can out of the auditorium we already have?

Perhaps I would feel differently about the planned auditorium if I were not so worried about its budget. But I see many, many problems with the plan for paying for this new auditorium. First, the budget relies too much on borrowing. We talk about educating our children for the future. But is taking on so much debt good for their future? I don't think so. Second, the budget seems to be too optimistic. Do we really think that building an auditorium can cost so little? Plus, I have never heard of a construction project that has been completed without going over its budget. Third, the budget does not account for the ongoing costs of <u>maintaining</u> an auditorium. What will it cost to heat and light this new space, for example? What will it cost to insure it?

5   Based on the budget, it does not look as if the school board has thought hard enough or clearly enough about its plan. Too many questions are unanswered. In the Westville public schools, our children are getting an excellent education, including a strong arts program. Let's not put our ability to keep paying for such an education at risk by spending our money foolishly now. Please vote no on the proposed school budget.

Kind regards,

Geoffrey Parker

8. Which is MOST LIKELY a reason why the author of this letter may be biased against the auditorium?

   A. He is a member of the school board.

   B. He has very little interest in music and the other arts.

   C. He does not have a child in the Westville public school system.

   D. He believes that his son's college is in greater need of an auditorium.

9. The use of the word <u>nevertheless</u> in paragraph 3 signals that the idea that follows will

   A. give a contrast.

   B. add to what came before.

   C. describe an effect.

   D. provide supporting details.

10. The word <u>maintaining</u> in paragraph 4 means

    A. paying for.

    B. keeping.

    C. completing.

    D. powering.

11. Which of the following is an example of the evidence the author gives to support his claim that "it does not look as if the school board has thought hard enough or clearly enough about its plan"?

    A. "Both of our children attended public schools, and both of our children learned to play instruments in the public schools."

    B. "The greater part of their arts education occurs in much smaller settings, such as the classroom."

    C. "Second, the budget seems to be too optimistic. Do we really think that building an auditorium can cost so little?"

    D. "In the Westville public schools, our children are getting an excellent education, including a strong arts program."

Use "Yes to the Auditorium!" and "No to the Auditorium!" to answer questions 12–14.

12. The authors of both letters hope to appeal to

    A. schoolchildren.

    B. parents of schoolchildren.

    C. the entire community.

    D. musicians and other performers.

13. How are the concerns of the author of the letter against the planned auditorium different from those of the authors of the letter in favor of it?

    A. He is more concerned about costs.

    B. He is not concerned about educating children.

    C. He is not concerned about space for performances.

    D. He is more concerned about his own family.

14. Both letters argue for a different thing. But, there is one thing that each letter argues for that is similar. Describe what is similar in the letters' arguments.

_____

_____

_____

_____

Read the story and answer the questions that follow.

Skate On

1   Dolores skated across the ice with practiced ease, zipping around other skaters as she picked up speed. It was a cool October night, and the rink in the park was filled with the chatter and laughter of dozens of skaters.

"Watch it!" someone yelled at Dolores as she zigzagged between two kids skating with their mom.

"Don't worry, I know what I'm doing!" she yelled over her shoulder.

Since she began skating as a five-year-old, Dolores had dreamed of winning gold one day as an Olympic speed skater, and even during a relaxed family skate, her desire for an increasing acceleration could <u>get the better of her</u>.

5   "Dolores!" her friend Celia called out as Dolores skated past her.

Dolores slowed down and waited for Celia to catch up. "You skate like my grandmother!" Dolores joked.

"We don't all skate like an out-of-control train, you know," Celia said, rolling her eyes. "You need to be a little more careful."

"I've fallen many times before, and it's really no big deal. Hey, Kim said she was going to be here, but I haven't seen her."

"Well, I haven't seen her, either," Celia said, scowling, "and I don't know why you hang out with her anyway. She acts so condescending as if she's better than everyone, just because her parents have a big house and buy her everything she wants . . ."

10   "Oh, come on, you're not starting that again, are you?" Dolores interrupted, feeling a <u>twinge</u> of guilt at the same time. Since Kim moved to town, Dolores had been spending more and more time with Kim and less and less time with Celia. Celia was her oldest, dearest friend, but like Dolores, Kim dreamed of competing in the Olympics one day as a speed skater.

"Hey, there's Kim!" Dolores shouted, pointing at a red-haired girl on the other side of the rink. Racing to catch up with her friend, Dolores just missed colliding with a little boy who fell down in front of her. She did a quick half-turn, then felt a sharp burst of pain in her ankle, collapsed onto the ice, and grabbed her ankle in agony.

"Get my parents, Celia!" she cried.

At the hospital, Dolores watched tearfully as the doctor wrapped her ankle and said she would need to be off her feet for two weeks.

"Am I going to be able to skate in two weeks?" Dolores asked.

15   "You'll be able to walk in two weeks," the doctor said, shaking her head, "but your ankle will still be healing. When you come back in two weeks, I'll have a better idea of when you can start skating again, but I should warn you that it could be months before you fully <u>recover</u>."

Go On ▶

"Months?" Dolores implored, feeling as if her world was crashing down around her.

"The time will fly by, you'll see," encouraged her dad, putting his arm around her.

That night, Dolores dreamed that she was skating in the Olympics. She saw herself slip, fall, and slide across the ice, knocking down two other skaters. Dolores woke in a panic, her heart pounding. What if her injury prevented her from ever skating again?

The next morning, Celia paid Dolores a visit.

20   "I brought you a book. It's the first of a trilogy that I think you'll like."

"Thanks," Dolores said, without raising her eyes.

Over the next week, Celia came every day, to play cards, tell jokes, and bring magazines and homemade cookies. Finally one morning, while they shared some hot chocolate, Dolores said, "Kim hasn't come by once, but you've been here every day."

"You're going to skate again, Dolores," Celia said, smiling, "and when you're skating for gold one day, I'm going to be right there in the front row, cheering you on."

Go On ▶

1. Which of the following is the BEST summary of this story?

   A. One October night, Dolores is at the skating rink, zipping past the other skaters. Her friend Celia calls out her name, and Dolores slows down to talk to her. They talk about Kim, whom Celia does not like. Suddenly, Dolores falls and sprains her ankle. Celia visits her at home.

   B. Dolores is skating at the rink in the park. Since she first learned to skate as a five-year-old, she has dreamed of winning an Olympic gold medal in speed skating. When she falls and sprains her ankle, Dolores fears her dream may never come true.

   C. Dolores loves to ice skate and dreams of winning gold in the Olympics. One day, she runs into her friend Celia at the skating rink. They talk until Dolores sees her friend Kim. Dolores speeds up to catch up with her friend, but she falls and sprains her ankle. She has to stay off her foot for two weeks.

   D. Dolores dreams of being an Olympic speed skater. She has been spending more time with a new friend, Kim, than with her longtime friend, Celia. One night Dolores badly sprains her ankle while skating. Celia visits her every day at home, and the girls' friendship is renewed.

2. The way the narrator portrays Dolores in paragraphs 1–3 could BEST be described as

   A. mean.

   B. clumsy.

   C. careless.

   D. selfish.

3. In paragraph 4, the statement that Dolores's "desire for an increasing acceleration could get the better of her" means that

   A. her skating improved as she went faster and faster.

   B. she often fell down when she went faster and faster.

   C. her desire to go faster and faster usually went away.

   D. she could lose control of her desire to go faster and faster.

4. In paragraph 10, twinge refers to a sudden feeling of

   A. pain.

   B. impatience.

   C. anger.

   D. confusion.

Go On ▶

5. As it is used in paragraph 15, <u>recover</u> means
   A. to wait.
   B. to get better.
   C. to be hidden.
   D. to practice.

6. What is the MAIN reason that Celia dislikes Kim?
   A. Kim lives in a big house.
   B. Kim gets everything she wants.
   C. Kim is a better skater than Celia.
   D. Kim sees Dolores more than Celia does.

7. What does this story show about true friendship? Use details from the story to support your answer.

_____

_____

_____

Read the story and answer the questions that follow.

Who Needs Roger?

1   "Hey, is something the matter?" Mark's mother was staring at him, her brow furrowed with concern.

"I guess I'm just not that hungry," Mark said, shrugging his shoulders and putting down his fork. Usually, he loved their lazy Saturday morning breakfasts of scrambled eggs and hot buttered toast, but today his stomach felt queasy, and the most he could do was push the food around on his plate. Meanwhile, he couldn't get his best friend's words out of his mind.

"I'm sorry, I can't hang out tomorrow," Roger had said after school the day before. "The tournament's in just two weeks, so I've got chess practice again. Maybe you can see if that new kid wants to hang out with you. You know, that kid who moved just down the street from you."

He must not want to be my friend anymore, Mark thought. Why else would Roger suggest that he go find someone else to go along with him on his aimless weekend excursions to the park? Mark tried to remember the last time they had done anything together. Just a few weeks ago, they had worked together on a <u>geology</u> project for school, which had involved hours of hunting for geodes and whatever other interesting rocks they could find. Since then, however, Roger had been spending all of his time practicing with the chess team and by now had probably decided he liked those guys better than Mark, who could not tell a pawn from a knight from a rook.

5   "It's too bad you can't see Roger today," said Mark's mom, as though she could read his mind. "Why don't you go introduce yourself to that kid who just moved down the street?"

"That's what Roger said I should do," said Mark, sighing.

"Well then, why not?" asked his mother, and so a half hour later, he found himself riding his bike down the street toward the new kid's house.

The new kid's name was James, and, as it turned out, he liked baseball and basketball and, like Mark, had no interest whatsoever in chess. Together, they biked to the park and played some basketball one-on-one. After a week of rain, it felt good to be running around in the warm spring sunshine, and Mark almost forgot about Roger.

"See you tomorrow?" James asked before he went home that afternoon.

10   "Yeah, sure," said Mark, silently adding to himself, *Who needs Roger?*

But when the doorbell rang the next morning, it was Roger standing on the doorstep, not James.

"What, no chess practice?" Mark asked.

"No, of course not," said Roger. "We never have practice on Sundays. Can I come in?" Roger walked into the den and plopped down on the couch, just as he did every time he was over at Mark's house. "What do you want to do today?" he asked.

Go On ▶

"Actually, I was thinking I would hang out with my *new friend*, James," said Mark. "Anyway, I didn't think you wanted to hang out with me anymore."

15   "Where'd you get an idea like that?"

"From the fact that after weeks of not hanging out all that much, if at all, you told me that I should go find a new friend."

"Well, I am with the chess team a lot, so I thought you might want someone else to hang out with when I'm not around. It's not like you can't have more than one friend."

Roger spoke in his usual matter-of-fact manner, but the words hit Mark like a kick in the gut. "You're right, I'm sorry," he said. "I guess I've just been missing you."

"Hey, <u>we all make mistakes</u>," said Roger. "So, what do you think—should we call James?"

Go On ▶

8. Which word BEST describes Roger as he is portrayed in this story?

   A. lonely

   B. confused

   C. insensitive

   D. reasonable

9. The Greek suffix -*logy*, as in geology in paragraph 4, means

   A. the study of.

   B. the search for.

   C. the memory of.

   D. the work on.

10. In paragraph 19, when Roger says that "we all make mistakes," you can conclude that

    A. he wants Mark to apologize again.

    B. he thinks that Mark made a terrible mistake.

    C. he is not bothered that Mark was angry with him.

    D. he made a mistake that he has not told Mark about.

11. Read this sentence from the story.

    "So, what do you think—should we call James?"

    How will Mark's reaction to this question MOST LIKELY compare with his reaction to Roger's similar suggestion at the beginning of the story?

    A. Mark is likely to get upset with Roger all over again.

    B. Mark is likely to be happy this time to include a new friend.

    C. Mark is likely to decide that he prefers spending time with James.

    D. Mark is likely to worry that Roger would rather hang out with James.

Go On ▶

12. Which BEST states a theme of this story?

   A. True friendship is neither selfish nor limited.

   B. Best friends do not stay best friends for long.

   C. Harmony between two friends is easier than among three.

   D. Friends with different interests lose interest in each other.

Use "Skate On" and "Who Needs Roger?" to answer question 13.

13. Why does Roger see James differently than Celia sees Kim? Use details from the stories to support your answer.

   _____

   _____

   _____

Go On ▶

Read the poem and answer the questions that follow.

Velvet Shoes
by Elinor Wylie

Let us walk in the white snow
In a soundless space;
With footsteps quiet and slow,
At a <u>tranquil</u> pace,
5   Under veils of white lace.

I shall go shod in silk[1],
And you in wool,
White as white cow's milk,
More beautiful
10   Than the breast of a <u>gull</u>.

We shall walk through the still town
In a windless peace;
We shall step upon white down,
Upon silver fleece,
15   Upon softer than these.

We shall walk in velvet shoes:
Wherever we go
Silence will fall like dews
On white silence below.
20   We shall walk in the snow.

[1]**shod in silk** wearing silk shoes

Go On ▶

14. When the speaker refers to "veils of white lace" in line 5, she is MOST LIKELY speaking about

    A. sheep.

    B. curtains.

    C. the snow.

    D. her shoes.

15. Read this entry from a thesaurus.

> **tranquil** *adjective.* peaceful
>
> Synonyms: calm, quiet, serene
>
> Antonyms: chaotic, loud, noisy, wild

Based on this entry, you can conclude that another word in the first stanza that means about the SAME as <u>tranquil</u> in line 4 is

    A. walk.

    B. white.

    C. soundless.

    D. slow.

16. Based on the context in the second stanza, you can conclude that a <u>gull</u> is a kind of

    A. tree.

    B. food.

    C. house.

    D. animal.

17. Read lines 11 and 12 from the poem.

> **We shall walk through the still town**
> **In a windless peace;**

From these lines, what can you infer about the speaker and her companion?

    A. They are alone outdoors.

    B. They have no home of their own.

    C. They are looking for a place to rest.

    D. They are unhappy with each other.

Go On ▶

18. How does the last stanza bring the poem to a satisfying conclusion?

    A. The pattern of rhymes changes.

    B. Another voice answers the speaker.

    C. The speaker makes a prediction about spring.

    D. The last line echoes the first line of the poem.

19. How does the speaker feel about the snow? Use images or words from the poem to support your answer.

    _____

    _____

    _____

Go On ▶

Read the passage and answer the questions that follow.

Recess: A Necessity, Not a Privilege

As explained in the following letter to the editor, the principal of Belleview Middle School has banned recess at the school. People in the community have different opinions on this ban. The editor of the school newspaper has published letters both for and against the ban. The following letter is against the ban.

Dear Editor:

1   As a fellow student in Belleview Middle School, you are no doubt aware of the incident that occurred during recess last week. Two students got into a fight during a flag football game. Because of that incident, the principal has banned after-lunch recess indefinitely. Maybe recess will start again next week, or next month—or maybe recess will be banned for the rest of the year. In the meantime, students will have to spend their after-lunch break in the cafeteria or auditorium. I respect the principal's right to make this decision. However, I disagree with this decision. In fact, based on conversations with my fellow students, in which I hear the same complaints again and again, I can say that we are all <u>unified</u> in our belief that Mr. Morris should immediately lift the ban on after-lunch recess.

First of all, we should remember that there are clear benefits to recess. Without recess, students are stuck indoors for hours at a time, which is not good for our health. We need fresh air, even if it's for only fifteen to twenty minutes during recess. Also, as health experts remind us everywhere in the media, we need exercise. How much exercise are we going to get sitting in a cafeteria or auditorium? Recess gives us the time to move our legs, run around, and just be active. Not only is this activity good for the body, but it's good for the mind. Students return to class re-energized and in a better mood.

<u>Moreover</u>, don't just take my word for it. Listen to the results of a study by researchers at Albert Einstein College of Medicine. They found that third graders with a daily recess of 15 minutes or longer learned better. They also found that the third graders with recess behaved better in the classroom. In other words, if your goal in banning recess is better-behaved students, the ban is likely to backfire. This study was published in 2009 in *Pediatrics,* which is the official journal of the American Academy of Pediatrics. This group of doctors agrees on the importance of recess. They have issued a policy statement that says that "recess is a crucial and necessary component of a child's development and, as such, it should not be withheld for punitive or academic reasons."

Go On ▶

Finally, it is completely unfair to punish all students for the actions of two. Only two students participated in the fight. The rest of the students in our school did nothing wrong. In fact, it was a student who alerted the recess monitor about the fight. Why should all students go without recess just because they happen to attend this school?

5   I've heard some say that recess is a privilege, not a right. I disagree. For the reasons I've given above, I say that recess is not a privilege, but a necessity. It is necessary for our health, both physical and mental. Mr. Morris has always been reasonable. I hope that he will recognize that banning after-lunch recess is both unjust and unhealthy.

Sincerely,

Skylar Cambria, Eighth Grader

Belleview Middle School

Go On ▶

20. Which is MOST LIKELY the reason why Skylar quotes a statement from the American Academy of Pediatrics in paragraph 3?

   A. to show that a group of experts would agree with him

   B. to show that adults do not understand what children really want

   C. to show that recess needs to be only 15 minutes long

   D. to show that a recess ban is a reasonable way to punish students

21. In paragraph 1, the word <u>unified</u> means that the students

   A. are determined.

   B. are of one mind.

   C. have many ideas.

   D. have no opinions.

22. The use of the word <u>moreover</u> in paragraph 3 signals that the ideas that follow will

   A. change the topic.

   B. give additional support.

   C. state an objection.

   D. tell about a contrasting idea.

23. Using information from the letter as evidence, explain what Skylar's main purpose is in writing this letter.

   _____

   _____

   _____

Practice Test 1

Go On ▶

Read the passage and answer the questions that follow.

Recess: A Privilege to Be Earned

The following letter is in support of the principal's ban on recess at Belleview Middle School.

Dear Editor:

1   I was shocked to learn about the fight that occurred during recess at Belleview Middle School last week. According to what I've heard, as many as a dozen or more students were involved. A fight like this one really ought to be called a brawl. Some claim that fewer students were involved, but why are they making excuses for such troublemakers? Any amount of fighting is a disgrace. Therefore, I write in full support of the <u>current</u> ban on recess at the school.

        Both of my children attended Belleview Middle School, the younger one graduating to the high school ten years ago. In the eight years that I had a child at the school, I never heard of any such fights breaking out among the students. Indeed, it certainly appears that today's youth are not what they used to be. In the newspapers and on TV, I regularly see reports on such troubling trends as bullying, both on the playground and on the Internet. These reports confirm what I regularly see on our city buses, in grocery stores, and at the local mall, where the children I encounter tend to be noisy and rude. Truly, I fear for the future.

        In the face of such problems, the withholding of such privileges as recess seems more than reasonable. If students cannot behave properly during recess, then they should have no recess. Some say that recess itself is the best time to learn how to behave during recess. I say that this reasoning is nonsense. Common sense shows that one learns how to do something *before* one does it, not *while* one does it. Thus, before any ban on recess is lifted, children should receive lessons on proper conduct. These lessons should address such subjects as etiquette and conflict resolution.

        I have also heard others cite experts, including the American Academy of Pediatrics, in support of recess. According to these experts, recess is necessary for the mental and physical health of today's students. But again, I turn to common sense. The school day is hardly more than six hours long. Am I to believe that in the remaining eighteen hours of the day, children are unable to find the time to run and play outdoors?

Go On ▶

5   After all, school time really ought to be time for learning rather than time for play. The world is becoming an ever more challenging place to earn a living. Today's children will be competing for jobs not just with their local peers, but with their peers around the globe. Given this situation, it would be better for children to focus on reading, writing, and mathematics during school hours. This way, they will be better prepared to face the future.

I commend Mr. Morris for his bold step in eliminating recess at Belleview Middle School. Perhaps students will show they deserve the right to have a break in the day. At that time, a lifting of the ban would be <u>fine</u>. In the meantime, students may find that they are benefiting from the extra time they now have for their studies.

Sincerely,

Frederick Gregorson, concerned citizen

Go On ▶

24. Read this entry from a dictionary.

> **cur•rent** *adjective*. **1:** happening now; **2:** popular, (in fashion) the current style; *noun*. **3:** a flowing, as of a river or of the air; **4:** the speed at which something flows

Which definition BEST explains the meaning of <u>current</u> in paragraph 1?

A. definition 1

B. definition 2

C. definition 3

D. definition 4

25. Based on the details in the letter, why might the author have a flawed opinion of the ban?

A. He is a good friend of Principal Morris.

B. He gets information about children only from the news.

C. He was once a victim of bullying.

D. He is a teacher who gives lessons on proper conduct.

26. What can be inferred from the author's statement "According to what I've heard, as many as a dozen or more students were involved" in the fight at Belleview Middle School?

A. The author of the letter enjoys gossiping.

B. The fight was large, involving many children.

C. The author of the letter has little direct knowledge about the fight.

D. The fight was typical of those that break out at the school.

27. In which of the following sentences does the word <u>fine</u> mean about the SAME as it means in paragraph 6?

A. Yesterday I felt ill, but today I feel fine.

B. If you get caught littering here, you will have to pay a fine.

C. My sister's hair is very thick, but mine is quite fine.

D. They will fine us and tow our car if we try to park it here.

Go On ▶

Use "Recess: A Necessity, Not a Privilege" and "Recess: A Privilege to Be Earned" to answer questions 28 and 29.

28. Which BEST compares the organization of "Recess: A Necessity, Not a Privilege" and "Recess: A Privilege to Be Earned"?

    A. In both letters, children's behavior is described as a problem.

    B. In both letters, the ban on recess is described as a solution.

    C. In "Recess: A Necessity, Not a Privilege," the ban on recess is described as a problem, whereas in "Recess: A Privilege to Be Earned," children's behavior is described as a problem.

    D. In "Recess: A Necessity, Not a Privilege," the ban on recess is described as a solution, whereas in "Recess: A Privilege to Be Earned," the ban on recess is described as a problem.

29. Which of the two letters do you think is more persuasive? Give two examples to support your response.

_____

_____

_____

Go On ▶

Read the story and answer the questions that follow.

The Jellyfish and the Monkey

1 Long ago, Jellyfish had bones and hard shells on their backs. This is the story of how the jellyfish became the creature we know today.

MY WIFE, THE QUEEN, IS GRAVELY ILL. **WHAT CAN WE DO?**

ONLY **THE LIVER OF A LIVE MONKEY** WILL SAVE HER.

2 JELLYFISH, GO TO THE LAND AND BRING ME A MONKEY AND HIS LIVER. YOU MUST SAVE OUR QUEEN. ONLY YOU CAN SAVE HER SINCE YOU HAVE LEGS TO WALK ON LAND.

I AM HONORED, BUT HOW WILL I CONVINCE A MONKEY TO RETURN WITH ME?

3 TELL HIM OF THE WONDERS OF THE SEA AND DESCRIBE THE LUXURY OF MY PALACE. GO, NOW. **YOU MUST HURRY!**

4

9 | BACK ON LAND

10 | DEFEATED, JELLYFISH RETURNS TO THE SEA KING'S PALACE.

11

12 | THAT DAY, THE JELLYFISH LOST HIS SHELL AND HIS BONES. FROM THEN ON, ALL JELLYFISH WERE BORN WITHOUT BONES AND SHELLS AND HAVE REMAINED NOTHING BUT JELLY TO THIS DAY.

30. What do the details in panels 1 and 2 emphasize about the setting of the story?

 A. The setting is underwater.

 B. The setting is in the future.

 C. The setting is in a castle.

 D. The setting is dangerous.

31. The word <u>convince</u> includes the Latin prefix *con-,* which means "with." Based on this information, you can conclude that <u>convince</u> in panel 2 means

 A. make with.

 B. go to stay with.

 C. replace with.

 D. persuade to agree with.

32. The word <u>luxury</u> includes the Latin root *luxus,* which means "extra, excess, extravagance." Based on this information, you can conclude that <u>luxury</u> in panel 3 means

 A. basic necessity.

 B. happiness and fun.

 C. underwater location.

 D. comfort and elegance.

33. Read this entry from a dictionary.

 store (stohr) *noun.* **1:** a place where things are sold; **2:** a supply of something; *verb.* **3:** to keep or hoard; *adjective.* **4:** bought from a store

 What part of speech is <u>store</u> as it is used in panel 8?

 A. noun

 B. verb

 C. adjective

 D. adverb

Practice Test 1

Go On ▶

34. What does the picture in panel 11 show?

    A. the jellyfish running away

    B. the jellyfish getting tricked

    C. the jellyfish losing its shell and bones

    D. the jellyfish fighting with the monkey

35. Using evidence from the story, explain how the jellyfish and monkey are DIFFERENT.

_____

_____

_____

Go On ▶

Read the passage and answer the questions that follow.

How Telescopes Work

1   In 1609, the Italian astronomer Galileo became the first person to point a telescope toward the heavens. He was not the first to make and use a telescope, but the telescopes he made were far better than those that came before. His telescopes could magnify an image up to 20 times. Also, before Galileo, no one had used a telescope to look at the sky. With his telescopes, Galileo observed craters on the moon, spots on the sun, moons revolving around Jupiter, and stars that had never been seen before.

    In the four hundred years since, telescopes have become more and more powerful. In fact, the James Webb Space Telescope, expected to begin working in 2018, will be able to collect light from the farthest reaches of the universe. The images we see through such telescopes continue to <u>reveal</u> much about the size, <u>makeup</u>, and beginnings of the universe. How do telescopes make it possible for us to see so much?

Optical Telescopes

    A telescope is a tool that is designed to collect light and make a magnified image. An **optical telescope** makes an image from visible light. Parts of an optical telescope include the *objective*, which collects and focuses light, and the *eyepiece,* which is used to see the image.

    The three basic types of optical telescopes each have a different kind of objective.

5   The **refracting telescope** is the type of telescope with which most people are familiar. It uses a lens or a group of lenses as the objective. The lenses are typically placed at the front of a tube. The lenses bend the light entering the tube, pointing the light toward a single point called the *focus.* The lenses in the eyepiece, usually found at the back of the tube, magnify the light from the focus. As a result, the viewer can clearly see an object that with the naked eye might appear blurred or faint.

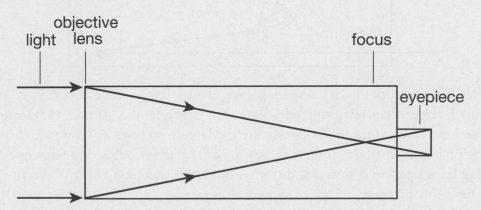

Go On ▶

The English physicist Isaac Newton invented the **reflecting telescope** sometime around 1680. This type of telescope uses a mirror instead of lenses as the objective. The mirror is typically placed at the back of the tube of the telescope. There, it collects light and reflects it back toward a focus. A secondary mirror placed within the path of the focus reflects some of the light to the side, toward the eyepiece. The eyepiece is typically mounted on the side of the tube.

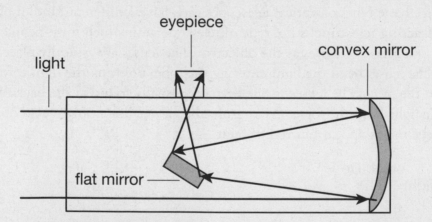

Reflecting telescopes have a few advantages over refracting telescopes. First, they can be made much larger than refracting telescopes. For example, the 40-inch (1.02 meters) lenses of the Yerkes Observatory in Wisconsin are the largest ever made. Compare those with the 315- or 394-inch (8 or 10 meters) mirrors of the largest reflecting telescopes! Second, refracting telescopes tend to create distorted images with a halo effect. Reflecting telescopes do not have this problem.

The third basic type of optical telescope is called a **compound** or **catadioptric** telescope. This type of telescope is a <u>hybrid</u>. It includes both lenses and mirrors. A German astronomer named Bernhard Schmidt made the first compound telescope in 1930.

Go On ▶

Non-optical telescopes

Most light, or electromagnetic radiation, is not visible to humans. This radiation includes radio waves, infrared light, ultraviolet light, X-rays, and gamma rays. **Non-optical telescopes** collect and record data from these kinds of radiation. The Webb Space Telescope is an example of a non-optical telescope. It will mostly collect and record data from infrared light. Its predecessor, the Hubble Space Telescope, is also a non-optical telescope. It collects ultraviolet and infrared light, as well as some visible light.

10   Thanks to the Hubble Space Telescope, we have seen the formation of galaxies. We have learned what the bright and distant objects called quasars really are. We have also discovered that mysterious dark energy fills the universe. What discoveries will the Webb telescope bring?

Go On ▶

36. Why does the author begin the passage by telling about Galileo?

    A. He invented the very first telescopes in 1609.

    B. His telescopes were the most powerful ones ever made.

    C. He was the first person to use telescopes for the purposes of astronomy.

    D. He used telescopes to make discoveries more amazing than any made since.

37. As it is used in paragraph 2, <u>reveal</u> means

    A. show.

    B. change.

    C. create.

    D. develop.

38. Read this entry from a dictionary.

> **make•up** *noun.* **1:** cosmetics, such as lipstick; **2:** the way something is put together; **3:** the method or process of laying something out, such as the pages of a publication; **4:** an assignment or test given in place of one that a student missed or failed

Which definition BEST explains the meaning of <u>makeup</u> in paragraph 2?

    A. definition 1

    B. definition 2

    C. definition 3

    D. definition 4

39. Based on the context in paragraph 8, you can conclude that the word <u>hybrid</u> refers to something that

    A. solves problems.

    B. is the best of its kind.

    C. is the last to be developed.

    D. combines different elements.

Go On ▶

40. What is MOST LIKELY the purpose of the diagrams that accompany this passage?

  A. to show how to use a telescope

  B. to show why reflecting telescopes are better

  C. to show how to make a telescope

  D. to show the paths of light through telescopes

41. Paragraph 7 mostly tells about

  A. causes and effects.

  B. problems and solutions.

  C. comparisons and contrasts.

  D. events in the order they happened.

42. Using details from the passage, explain two of the main ways in which refracting and reflecting telescopes are DIFFERENT from each other.

_____

_____

_____

Go On ▶

Read the passage and answer the questions that follow.

Gazing at the Distant Past: Quasars

1   As telescopes have gotten more powerful, they have helped us discover many new mysteries in the universe. Fortunately, these telescopes have also been able to help us solve many of these same mysteries. The superbright, superdistant objects called quasars are one of these mysteries.

Discovering the Mystery

In the 1960s, astronomers began to locate powerful sources of radio waves. These radio sources were points of light, similar to stars. Because of their starlike appearance, astronomers called them *quasi-stellar objects,* or *quasars.*

However, quasars could not possibly be stars. They are billions of <u>light-years</u> away, much too far away for a single star to be seen, even with a telescope. To be visible at such a great distance, a quasar would have to be much, much brighter than a star. In fact, quasars can be as bright as *billions* of stars together. A single quasar is as bright as an entire galaxy— but no larger than our solar system. How can this be?

Solving the Mystery

In the 1980s, astronomers took a closer look at the halos that surround some quasars. They discovered that these halos are actually the faint images of galaxies surrounding the quasars. In other words, a quasar is a powerful source of energy at the center of a galaxy.

5   After this discovery, astronomers came up with a theory that is now widely believed to be true. This theory proposes that quasars are actually giant black holes. Each of these black holes is found at the center of a galaxy, where stars are closest together. The strong gravity of the black hole draws stars toward it, tearing them apart. It is the extremely hot gases of these torn-apart stars that produce the powerful, bright energy emitted by a quasar.

Go On ▶

This theory accounts for both parts of the mystery of quasars. First, it explains why a quasar is so bright. Second, it explains why a quasar takes up a relatively small region of space. One of the basic characteristics of black holes is their density. Though they are massive, they are also compact. Like tightly packed suitcases, they squeeze a vast amount of mass into a tiny space. But this space is much, much smaller than a suitcase, and it holds a lot more. Think of the entire mass of a star squeezed down to the size of an atom!

Clues about the Past

In 2000 and 2002, astronomers identified quasars located about 13 billion light-years away. The light that we observe from these quasars left 13 billion years ago, when the universe was still very young. To study these quasars, therefore, is to study the distant past.

What have we learned about the past from the study of quasars? For one thing, we have found that quasars were once more common than they are now. In general, the farther one looks toward the edges of the universe—and therefore the deeper one looks into the past—the more quasars one finds. Beyond about 10 billion light-years, though, fewer quasars can be found. It appears that it took some time after the formation of the universe for the quasar population to build up.

In the future, the study of quasars is likely to reveal even more about the early years of the universe, including how galaxies form.

Go On ▶

43. Which of the following is the BEST summary of this passage?

    A. Quasars are bright and distant objects that astronomers have yet to understand.

    B. Discovered in the 1960s, quasars are now thought to be giant black holes at the centers of distant galaxies.

    C. Although quasars are each as bright as an entire galaxy, they are not any larger than the solar system.

    D. The study of quasars is likely to result in better understanding of the formation of galaxies.

44. In paragraph 3, <u>light-years</u> are units of

    A. time.

    B. mass.

    C. distance.

    D. brightness.

45. Paragraph 5 mostly tells about

    A. the effects of the causes described in paragraphs 2 and 3.

    B. the explanation of the mystery described in paragraphs 2 and 3.

    C. the events that occurred after the events described in paragraphs 2 and 3.

    D. comparisons and contrasts with the ideas described in paragraphs 2 and 3.

46. What does paragraph 6 explain?

    A. the causes that tell why quasars appear as they do

    B. the problems with the theory that tells what quasars are

    C. the differences between quasars and stars

    D. the events leading up to our current understanding of quasars

Go On ▶

47. In paragraph 6, black holes are compared to tightly packed suitcases in order to explain

    A. how bright they are.

    B. how distant they are.

    C. how massive they are.

    D. how compact they are.

48. The author of this passage sees quasars as

    A. impossible to understand.

    B. beautiful, but not valuable.

    C. mysterious and fascinating.

    D. too far away to be interesting.

Use "How Telescopes Work" and "Gazing at the Distant Past: Quasars" to answer questions 49 and 50.

49. Based on information in "How Telescopes Work," which of the following is MOST LIKELY the type of telescope that was used in discovering quasars?

    A. refracting telescope

    B. reflecting telescope

    C. compound telescope

    D. non-optical telescope

50. Why are telescopes important instruments in our understanding of quasars? Use details from both "How Telescopes Work" and "Gazing at the Distant Past: Quasars" to support your answer.

    _____

    _____

    _____

Read the passage and answer the questions that follow.

Comic Books: Fun for All Ages

1   It's late at night, the lights are out, and you should be sleeping. Instead, you're in bed with a flashlight, reading a comic book under the covers. If this describes you, you're not alone. Reading comic books in bed is a tradition that has been maintained by kids and the young at heart for decades. When did comic books—and this tradition—get their start?

The Yellow Kid

In 1892, a man named Richard F. Outcault moved to New York City to find work as an illustrator for magazines. Outcault was a trained and highly skilled artist whose drawings reflected his interest in urban life. The characters in his drawings were often tough, streetwise kids who kept their sense of humor and fun while surviving the rough streets of their neighborhoods.

In 1895, a newspaper called *New York World* began to publish *Hogan's Alley,* a cartoon by Outcault. The cartoon featured a bald-headed boy with big ears named Mickey Dugan. Dugan soon began to wear a long yellow shirt, and he became known as the Yellow Kid.

Hogan's Alley became wildly popular. Its portrayal of immigrant kids living in the city <u>appealed</u> to many readers, especially those who had moved to New York from other countries. It was so popular that a battle for control of the cartoon was waged between *New York World* and its rival newspaper, *New York Journal*. Publishers had realized that cartoons helped sell newspapers.

5   But *Hogan's Alley* did more than <u>generate</u> interest in newspaper funnies. It established features that would become standard in comic books. First, Outcault's cartoon had a regular cast of characters. Second, it told stories that were funny and entertaining. Third, and perhaps most importantly, the stories were told through a combination of words and pictures. Then, in "The Yellow Kid and His New Phonograph," published on October 25, 1896, the cartoon's story was presented in a series of panels. Outcault had invented the comic strip.

Go On ▶

After the Yellow Kid

There was a lot of money to be made from comic strips. During the early 1900s, many new strips appeared. These included *Buster Brown* (also by Outcault), *Mutt and Jeff*, and *The Katzenjammer Kids*.

Sometimes the individual comic strips were collected and published as a set. In 1933, two men working for a printing company came up with a <u>novel</u> idea. Max C. Gaines and Harry Wildenberg published a set of collected comic strips called *Funnies on Parade*. The book was folded in half and stapled in the middle like a magazine. It was sold at newsstands for ten cents a copy. This new format was so successful that the men began to publish a new collection each month. These collections of comic strips were the first true comic books.

Superheroes to the Rescue!

In 1938, the first comic book starring what is probably the most famous superhero of them all hit the newsstands. Created by Jerome Siegel and Joseph Shuster, the hero was Superman. The popularity of this character led to the creation of more superheroes. Comic books featuring Batman, Wonder Woman, the Flash, and Captain America were a great success. Then, in 1952, superheroes moved from the page to the screen. The first episode of *Adventures of Superman* was broadcast on television.

Comic Books Today

More than a century after Outcault's first comic strip, comic books have come of age. Such movies as *Superman* in 1978 and *Batman* in 1989 expanded the audience for comic book characters and their stories. In 2012, *The Avengers* became one of the highest-grossing movies of all time. At the same time, comic books have become a form in which artists take up serious stories, such as Art Spiegelman's *Maus,* which won a special Pulitzer Prize in 1992. What some once thought of as a medium for telling silly stories for kids has proven to fascinate just about everyone.

Go On ▶

1. Which BEST describes the overall text structure of this passage?

   A. cause and effect

   B. problem and solution

   C. compare and contrast

   D. chronological order

2. As it is used in paragraph 4, <u>appealed</u> means

   A. asked for help.

   B. interested or pleased.

   C. applied to a higher court.

   D. turned to someone for a decision.

3. As it is used in paragraph 5, <u>generate</u> means

   A. give.

   B. amuse.

   C. create.

   D. engage.

4. Read these entries from a dictionary.

   nov•el^1 (nä'-vəl) *noun.* **1.** a long work of fiction; **2.** *obs.* a short story or novella
   nov•el^2 (nä'-vəl) *adjective.* new, original
   nov•el^3 (nä'-vəl) *noun.* a change to an existing law

   Which definition BEST explains the meaning of <u>novel</u> in paragraph 7?

   A. entry 1, definition 1

   B. entry 1, definition 2

   C. entry 2

   D. entry 3

Go On ▶

5. Read this sentence.

> **Outcault took his cartoon to the *New York Journal*, which soon began to publish a Sunday comics section.**

In which section of the passage does this sentence MOST LIKELY belong?

A. the section titled "The Yellow Kid"

B. the section titled "After the Yellow Kid"

C. the section titled "Superheroes to the Rescue!"

D. the section titled "Comic Books Today"

6. Which statement BEST describes the author's point of view on comic books?

A. Comic books mostly tell silly stories for kids.

B. Comic books have something to offer everyone.

C. Comic books are the best medium for skilled artists.

D. Comic books today are better than those made in the past.

7. According to the passage, how did comic books grow from comic strips?

_____

_____

_____

Go On ▶

Read the passage and answer the questions that follow.

Will Eisner: A Life in Comics

1   Many people believe that Will Eisner is the most influential comic artist of all time. He is known as "the father of the graphic novel." Born in 1917 to Jewish immigrant parents, he came of age during the golden age of comics and continued to grow with them through the twentieth century, breaking boundaries and eventually inventing a new form.

Early Years

Eisner's father worked as a backdrop painter for the theater. His practical mother was not so interested in art. She worried that by pursuing comic book art, her son was wasting his time on a career that would come to nothing.

As a young man, Eisner got a job selling newspapers. Every day after work, he took some half-dozen newspapers home so he could read the funnies. Other early influences on his work were movies, "pulps," and stories written by Horatio Alger. Eisner later said, "Alger's message was that you can rise above your circumstances and find success through your own <u>diligence</u> and hard work. And as a kid in the ghetto, that spoke directly to me. And the stories were about an average person triumphing against obstacles, and that's a theme that I've returned to many times in my work. It was powerful stuff to me then. They still stick with me; they had a tremendous effect on me."

Partnership

In the 1930s, as a nineteen-year-old high school graduate, Eisner partnered with Jerry Iger to provide new material to comic book publishers. Eisner would create the material, and Iger would sell it to publishers. In this venture, Eisner hired and worked with some of the best names in comics, including Bob Kane, the creator of *Batman,* and Jack Kirby, the co-creator of *Spider-Man* and *The Fantastic Four*. At this time, Eisner himself created such comics as *Sheena, Queen of the Jungle* and *Hawks of the Seas.*

5   In this way, Eisner found both creative and financial success before he was even twenty-two years old. Indeed, his mother could let go of her worries about his career in comic books. With her husband out of work, her artist son was supporting the family. "My father was pleased that I was using my art to make a living," said Eisner, "and while my mother had no real aesthetic judgments, she was happy that I was doing well."

Go On ▶

The Spirit

Despite his success, Eisner was restless. In 1939, publisher Everett "Busy" Arnold approached him with the idea of creating a weekly comic book that would be distributed with the Sunday papers. For this Sunday section, Eisner created *The Spirit*.

The Spirit was a detective who worked outside the law. Because Arnold wanted Eisner to create a superhero like Superman or Batman, Eisner gave his character a mask and gloves. However, The Spirit had no superpowers. Eisner saw him as an "adventurer" whom he could put "in almost any situation." By inventing a character like this, Eisner gave himself the freedom to tell all kinds of stories. Over twelve years of creating *The Spirit*, Eisner played with language and genre, moving well beyond the bounds of what was expected in a detective story.

The Graphic Novel

In 1952, Eisner gave up *The Spirit* to focus on work for his company, American Visuals Corporation. With this company, he made comics and illustrations for educational and commercial purposes. He continued this work well into the 1970s.

But Eisner had not given up on telling stories for stories' sake. In 1978, in fact, he published something entirely new: the first graphic novel. *A Contract with God* was a literary novel in comic book form—and it was only the first of several such novels that Eisner worked on through the last decades of his life. Eisner died in 2005.

10   Today, the Eisner Award is one of the most prestigious awards in comics. Several books and a documentary film, *Will Eisner: Portrait of a Sequential Artist*, tell about his life and work.

Go On ▶

8. Which of the following is the BEST summary of this passage?

   A. Will Eisner's mother worried about his career, but it turned out that he found great success in comic books.

   B. Will Eisner created such memorable comic-book characters as Sheena, Queen of the Jungle and The Spirit.

   C. Will Eisner's remarkable career extended from the golden age of comic books through his own invention of graphic novels.

   D. Will Eisner created a new form, the graphic novel, with his publication of *A Contract with God* in 1978.

9. Will Eisner is MOST LIKELY known as "the father of the graphic novel" because he

   A. invented the graphic novel.

   B. had children who made graphic novels.

   C. predicted the creation of the graphic novel.

   D. taught others how to make graphic novels.

10. From the context in paragraph 3, you can conclude that the word <u>diligence</u> means

    A. great success.

    B. constant effort.

    C. difficult problems.

    D. inspiring message.

11. Read this sentence from the passage.

    Indeed, his mother could let go of her worries about his career in comic books. With her husband out of work, her artist son was supporting the family.

    Based on these statements, you can infer that

    A. Eisner's father was not interested in working for a living.

    B. most artists are able to earn enough to live on from making their art.

    C. people could make enough money working on comic books in the 1930s.

    D. Eisner worked on other jobs while also pursuing his work in comic books.

Go On ▶

12. Paragraph 7 mostly tells about

    A. the causes that affected Eisner's choices in creating The Spirit.

    B. the ways in which working on The Spirit solved some of Eisner's problems.

    C. events in the development of The Spirit in the order in which they happened.

    D. comparisons and contrasts between The Spirit and other comic book heroes.

13. How was Will Eisner's life like one of Horatio Alger's stories, as he describes them in paragraph 3?

    A. He found success through hard work.

    B. He was an average person who became a superhero.

    C. He made his way to the top because luck was on his side.

    D. His parents were obstacles to his making his dreams come true.

Use "Comic Books: Fun for All Ages" and "Will Eisner: A Life in Comics" to answer questions 14 and 15.

14. The biography of Will Eisner demonstrates which of the following ideas from "Comic Books: Fun for All Ages"?

    A. "Reading comic books in bed is a tradition that has been maintained by kids and the young at heart for decades."

    B. "These collections of comic strips were the first true comic books."

    C. "Comic books featuring Batman, Wonder Woman, the Flash, and Captain America were a great success."

    D. "At the same time, comic books have become a form in which artists take up serious stories."

15. What is one way that Will Eisner's work in comics shows the "coming of age" of comic books described in the conclusion of "Comic Books: Fun for All Ages"?

_____

_____

_____

Go On ▶

Read the story and answer the questions that follow.

As Dear as Salt

1 AS YOU KNOW, I NEED TO APPOINT ONE OF YOU TO BE MY SUCCESSOR TO THE THRONE. BUT, FIRST, YOU NEED TO PROVE YOUR WORTH. YOU HAVE ONE DAY TO BRING ME THE MOST INDISPENSABLE THING.

2 THE NEXT DAY

FATHER, I HAVE BROUGHT YOU THIS BEAUTIFUL, PURPLE ROBE. CLOTHING WILL KEEP YOU WARM. IT IS SURELY INDISPENSABLE.

3 FATHER, I HAVE BROUGHT YOU FOOD. BERRIES WILL NOURISH YOU. SURELY, THEY ARE THE MOST INDISPENSABLE THING.

4 FATHER, I HAVE BROUGHT YOU SALT. IT BRINGS FLAVOR TO EVERYTHING YOU EAT. WE CANNOT EAT WITHOUT IT.

5

SALT?! OUT OF MY PALACE NOW. SALT IS FIT ONLY FOR A PEASANT, NOT FOR ONE WHO SITS UPON THE THRONE!

6

NOW, FOR THE THRONE. PRINCESS, YOUR PURPLE ROBE IS THE COLOR OF KINGS. THAT IS THE MOST INDISPENSABLE THING. YOU WILL BE QUEEN.

7

I CAN'T BELIEVE MY LITTLE PRINCESS WOULD THINK OF SALT. HOW SILLY!

8

OUTSIDE THE KING'S PALACE

HELLO! I HAVE TRAVELED FAR TODAY. IN RETURN FOR A PLACE TO STAY, I WILL COOK.

INN

SURE! OUR COOK QUIT JUST YESTERDAY. WELCOME.

16. Based on the context in the story, you can conclude that the word <u>indispensable</u> in panel 1 means

   A. valuable.

   B. flavorful.

   C. necessary.

   D. disappointing.

17. Read this sentence from the story.

   Salt is fit only for a <u>peasant</u>, not for one who sits upon the throne!

   Based on the context in this sentence, you can conclude that the word <u>peasant</u> in panel 5 refers to someone who is

   A. thin and hungry.

   B. cheerful and polite.

   C. displeased and noisy.

   D. poor and unimportant.

18. What does the picture in panel 5 emphasize by focusing on the king's face?

   A. his desire to gain even more power

   B. his anger about his daughter's gift of salt

   C. his happiness with his first daughter's answer

   D. his sorrow about banishing his daughter

19. The word <u>requested</u> in panel 9 has the same root as the word *question*. Based on this information, you can conclude that <u>requested</u> means

   A. asked.

   B. spoken.

   C. learned.

   D. searched.

Go On ▶

20. What does the princess's time working as a cook show about her character?

    A. She can adapt to different ways of life.

    B. She would rather be a cook than the queen.

    C. She is stubborn and needs to prove she is right.

    D. She forgets about her family easily.

21. What does the reader learn about the princess's actions in the story?

    A. She enjoys disguising herself.

    B. She believes she is better than her sisters.

    C. She is good-natured in spite of her trouble.

    D. She thinks it is fun to live outside of the castle.

22. Which BEST states a theme of this story?

    A. Power tends to harm one's judgment.

    B. Clothing and food are not so important.

    C. Parents should listen to their children.

    D. Things that seem unimportant may be necessary.

23. Compare and contrast the king and the princess, based on their interactions in this story.

    _____

    _____

    _____

Go On ▶

Read the poem and answer the questions that follow.

The Violet
by Jane Taylor

Down in a green and shady bed
A modest violet grew;
Its stalk was bent, it hung its head,
As if to hide from view.

5   And yet it was a lovely flower,
Its colors bright and fair;
It might have <u>graced</u> a rosy bower[1]
Instead of hiding there.

Yet there it was <u>content</u> to bloom,
10   In modest tints arrayed[2]
And there <u>diffused</u> its sweet perfume,
Within the silent shade.

Then let me to the valley go,
This pretty flower to see,
15   That I may also learn to grow
In sweet humility.

[1]**bower** a shady resting place in a garden or park
[2]**In modest tints arrayed** dressed in modest colors

Go On ▶

24. The speaker's feelings about the violet could BEST be described as

A. amazed.

B. admiring.

C. annoyed.

D. confused.

25. Read lines 3 and 4 from the poem.

> Its stalk was bent, it hung
> its head,
> As if to hide from view.

From these lines, what can you infer about the violet?

A. It is confused.

B. It is dying.

C. It is plain.

D. It is humble.

26. Read this entry from a thesaurus.

> **grace** *verb.* to add grace to
>
> Synonyms: beautify, decorate, ornament
>
> Antonyms: damage, deform

Based on this entry, you can conclude that a word that means the OPPOSITE of <u>graced</u> in line 7 is

A. grew.

B. improved.

C. honored.

D. harmed.

27. Read this entry from a dictionary.

> **con•tent** (kuhn-tent') *adjective.*
> **1**: satisfied; *verb.* **2**: to make content; *noun.* **3**: contentment; the feeling of satisfaction

What part of speech is <u>content</u> as it is used in line 9?

A. noun

B. verb

C. adjective

D. adverb

Go On ▶

28. The word <u>diffused</u> includes the Latin prefix *dif-*, which means "opposite of, not," and the root *fuse,* which means "to bring together, unite." Based on this information, you can conclude that <u>diffused</u> in line 11 means

   A. spread.

   B. displayed.

   C. touched.

   D. joined.

29. What does the speaker think is MOST important about the violet?

   A. its beauty

   B. its sweet scent

   C. its modesty

   D. its living in a valley

30. How does the last stanza of the poem compare with the others?

   A. It tells about the speaker, whereas the others tell only about the violet.

   B. It describes the speaker's plans for the violet, whereas the others describe the violet's wishes.

   C. It explains why the speaker dislikes the violet, whereas the others praise it.

   D. It invites the reader to share thoughts about the violet, whereas the others share only the speaker's thoughts.

31. In two to three sentences, write a summary of the poem.

_____

_____

_____

Practice Test 2

Go On ▶

Read the passage and answer the questions that follow.

Recycling, At Last!

The town of Greenville has recently started a recycling program. After publishing an article about the program, the local newspaper has received letters expressing different opinions about it. The editor has published some of these letters. The following letter is in support of the program.

Dear Editor:

1   I read your June 20 article "Greenville Goes Green" with great delight. For years I have been ashamed of the lack of a recycling program in our town. With a heavy heart, I dropped used paper, glass jars, and plastic bottles in the trash. In other towns, I could have recycled these items. At last, thanks to the efforts of the students at Greenville Elementary School, I can put these things where they belong: in the recycling bin.

Unfortunately, many people <u>object</u> to the new recycling program. They do not like having to sort the things they are throwing away into three different bins, one for garbage, and two for recycling. Some say that the work of sorting takes too much time. Others say that the work is confusing—which items should go into which bins? For these people, I have some helpful tips.

First, I recommend that people sort the things they are throwing away as they throw them away. In other words, don't dump everything into one bin to sort out later, which is messy, smelly work anyway. Keep three bins in a place that is convenient. Ours are in the garage, just off of our kitchen. As we throw things away, we place them in the correct bin: garbage in the trash bin; paper and cardboard in the blue recycling bin; and cans, jars, bottles, and other plastic in the green recycling bin. Similarly, I now have two wastebaskets next to my desk. I use one for garbage and the other for paper to recycle.

Second, for those who find it confusing to sort their trash, I recommend that they use the handy fliers that the town has made. The fliers use pictures to show which kinds of items belong in each bin. In our home, we've posted a flier on the wall above the bins in our garage. If I'm ever uncertain whether or not an item can be recycled, I can just check the flier.

5   As you can see, in just ten days of recycling in Greenville, we've made it part of our regular household routine. I don't find myself working much harder to take care of our garbage than I did before! And I believe that taking a couple more bins to the curb on trash pick-up day is more than worth it. The article "Greenville Goes Green" noted the problem of overflowing landfills. Additionally, did you know that recycling results in reduced emissions of the greenhouse gases that are changing our climate? According to the Environmental Protection Agency, 85 million tons of waste were recycled or composted in 2010. As a result, more than 186 million metric tons of carbon dioxide equivalent emissions were kept out of the environment. This reduction is like taking 36 million passenger vehicles off the road.

Go On ▶

<u>Finally</u>, I would like to congratulate the students of Greenville Elementary School. It is thanks to their campaign that the town council got its act together and got a recycling program started. What an inspiration these children should be to all of us! If a group of children can work for three years to improve our community, I think that the rest of us can make the small effort to sort our trash.

Sincerely,

Sonia Perez

Go On ▶

32. Which BEST describes the overall organization of this passage?

    A. The author explains the positive effects of recycling.

    B. The author shares solutions for some problems people have recycling.

    C. The author compares life in Greenville before and after recycling.

    D. The author tells about events in the Greenville students' campaign in order.

33. In which of the following sentences does the word <u>object</u> mean about the SAME as it means in paragraph 2?

    A. My object in visiting is simply to cheer you up.

    B. The object was round like a ball but heavier than a rock.

    C. Will you object if I play some music while we wash dishes?

    D. The new piano was an object of curiosity to the preschoolers.

34. The use of the word <u>finally</u> in paragraph 6 signals that the ideas that follow will

    A. explain the main idea.

    B. introduce a new idea.

    C. give the concluding ideas.

    D. tell about a contrasting idea.

35. For what reason does the author of this article explain that the waste recycled or composted in 2010 was "like taking 36 million passenger vehicles off the road"?

_____

_____

_____

Go On ▶

Read the passage and answer the questions that follow.

Recycling: Just a Very Small Start

The following letter raises some concerns about the new recycling program in the town of Greenville.

Dear Editor:

1   I write in regard to your June 20 article "Greenville Goes Green." What an inspiring story! I am truly impressed with the students of Greenville Elementary School. They saw a problem, and for three years they did not stop their campaign for recycling until the town council voted to seek a new trash contractor. At last, Greenville has a recycling program. What a tribute to the efforts of our town's young citizens!

However, I feel I must speak out with my concerns about the spirit in which many people are taking up this new program. Yes, the start of recycling in our town is indeed cause for celebration. But as a solution to our world's environmental problems, recycling has its limits. We need to be doing much, much more than just dropping our used plastic bottles in a green bin.

On its own, recycling is no solution to the problems of overconsumption and waste. First, most of the items that we recycle are not recycled in the way that most of us probably imagine that they are—used plastic bottles becoming new plastic bottles, for example. It would be more accurate to say that these items are <u>downcycled</u>. In other words, they are made into products that are themselves not recycled, such as fleece jackets or carpeting. So much of what we recycle is not really kept out of the trash. It would be more accurate to say that the item's trip to the landfill is not avoided, but delayed.

Second, the recycling process itself is not without its problems. For example, most of our recycled plastics are actually shipped overseas. The export of these plastics results not only in the large <u>carbon footprint</u> associated with the shipping, but in the release of far more toxins into our environment. Processing plastic for re-use, like making new plastic, involves toxins, and the environmental standards in China, where most of our recycled plastic goes, are much lower than they are here.

5   Finally, there seems to be a belief that as long as you recycle your stuff, it's okay to buy as much stuff as you want. For the reasons I've given above, this belief is simply false. We need to do more—and we can do more. The students of Greenville Elementary School did not stop campaigning for recycling until they got recycling. I say, let's not stop with just recycling. Let's look for ways to help our environment by *reducing* what we use. Plastic bags, for example, are a menace. They blow away, get caught up in trees, clog up storm drains, and—worst of all—harm wildlife (especially marine animals) that mistake them for food. How about a local ban on plastic shopping bags?

Go On ▶

Perhaps people will laugh at the idea, thinking that our community would never do anything so extreme. But just think of how many people laughed at the Greenville students and their recycling campaign. As I said, they've inspired me. I think we can do more. What about you?

Sincerely,

Nancy Williams

36. Which quotation from the letter BEST expresses its main idea?

   A. "I am truly impressed with the students of Greenville Elementary School."

   B. "Yes, the start of recycling in our town is indeed cause for celebration."

   C. "On its own, recycling is no solution to the problems of overconsumption and waste."

   D. "How about a local ban on plastic shopping bags?"

37. Based on the comparison with the term *recycle* in paragraph 3, which BEST explains the meaning of the term downcycle?

   A. to send used items to the landfill

   B. to keep used items for different purposes

   C. to make similar new items out of used items

   D. to turn used items into new and sometimes different items

38. As it is used in paragraph 4, carbon footprint refers to

   A. the weight of carbon in a shipment.

   B. the use of carbon to recycle used plastics.

   C. the distance traveled in terms of carbon burned.

   D. the carbon dioxide emitted by a given activity.

39. Based on information in this letter, with which of these statements would the author MOST LIKELY agree?

   A. It is impossible to help the environment.

   B. Even good ideas can seem foolish at first.

   C. There is no value in recycling your waste.

   D. Today's youth are in need of inspiration.

Go On ▶

Use "Recycling, At Last!" and "Recycling: Just a Very Small Start" to answer questions 40 and 41.

40. Which BEST compares the text structure of "Recycling: Just a Very Small Start" with that of "Recycling, At Last!"?

    A. Unlike "Recycling, At Last!," "Recycling: Just a Very Small Start" tells mostly about problems, but not solutions.

    B. Like "Recycling, At Last!," "Recycling: Just a Very Small Start" tells about solutions without identifying the problem.

    C. Like "Recycling, At Last!," "Recycling: Just a Very Small Start" tells mostly about the effects of recycling.

    D. Unlike "Recycling, At Last!," "Recycling: Just a Very Small Start" tells about the causes leading to the start of recycling in Greenville.

41. In what ways do the authors of these two letters agree? Give two examples.

_____

_____

_____

Go On ▶

Read the drama and answer the questions that follow.

Hawk Watch

CAST OF CHARACTERS

LAUREN, a ten-year-old girl
BETH, Lauren's mom
AARON, Lauren's older brother
AUNT ZIVA

Scene 1

SETTING: *Nighttime. Moonlight shining dimly through a window to the side shows a small eat-in kitchen. A cell phone on the table begins to ring. Beth enters, wearing a nightgown, and answers the phone.*

1   BETH: Hello? (*pause*) Yes, Dad, I'm just about ready to go to bed. (*Another pause, and when Beth speaks again, she sounds shocked.*) What? (*She pulls out a chair and sits down.*) Do you need me to come help out? I can come now.... (*pause*) Are you sure she's OK? And what about you? (*pause*) OK. I took off work tomorrow, so it's not too hard to <u>adjust</u> my plans. I'll talk to Ziva, and we'll come over. (*pause*) Yes, I love you, too. And give Mom a big hug. (*pause*) Good-bye. (*Beth turns off the phone, puts it down, and sighs.*) Lauren is going to be so disappointed.

Scene 2

SETTING: *The same kitchen, early in the morning. Lauren and Aaron are eating breakfast. Lauren eats quickly, scooping large spoonfuls of cereal into her mouth and making loud crunching noises. Aaron watches with <u>amusement</u>.*

AARON: Whoa! Slow down there. You're eating like you're late for school or something. It's Saturday.

LAUREN: (*with cereal in her mouth*) I know what day it is. Did you forget? Mom's taking me to see the hawks in Corpus Christi today.

(*Aaron watches Lauren silently for a few moments before speaking.*)

AARON: Um ... are you sure about that?

5   LAUREN: Of course I'm sure. We planned it weeks ago. Mom took the day off and everything.

AARON: I know. But hasn't Mom told you ... (*pausing*)

Go On ▶

LAUREN: (*interrupting*) We've got the folding chairs in the back of the van, sunscreen, bug spray. I've got my binoculars. (*She taps a pair of binoculars on the table next to her cereal bowl.*) All we have to do is bring down the sandwiches and the cooler.

AARON: (*reluctantly*) I know how much you're looking forward to this, but I heard Mom talking on the phone last night after you went to bed. There's something you should know.

LAUREN: What? (*Beth enters, wearing a pretty print blouse and a skirt. Lauren watches as her mom pours herself a cup of coffee.*) Hey, Mom, <u>don't take this the wrong way</u>, but I think you should change your clothes. We're going to be sitting outside in a park watching hawks for a few hours. You'd be more comfortable in jeans and a T-shirt.

10   BETH: Lauren, I need to talk to you. (*The doorbell rings.*) That's probably your Aunt Ziva.

AARON: I'll get it.

LAUREN: (*smiling*) I didn't know she was coming! Is she going with us to Corpus Christi?

(*Beth sighs and puts her cup of coffee down. She sits next to Lauren at the table. Aunt Ziva enters with Aaron, who sits down to finish his breakfast. Aunt Ziva grins at Lauren and opens her arms for a hug. Lauren jumps up and hugs her aunt, a big smile on her face.*)

AUNT ZIVA: How's my favorite niece? OK, you're my only niece, but still my favorite!

LAUREN: I'm so happy you're here! Mom didn't tell me you were coming, too. You're going to love the hawk watch, Aunt Ziva. Every year at this time, thousands and thousands of migrating hawks go around the Gulf of Mexico. They fly during the day, riding warm air currents <u>like leaves blown by the wind</u>. I've never been able to go to the hawk watch to see them before. I can't wait! (*She slips her binoculars over her head.*) I think I have an extra pair of these, Aunt Ziva. I'll go get them for you.

(*Beth and Aunt Ziva exchange looks. Beth gets up and puts her hand on Lauren's shoulder.*)

15   BETH: Lauren, sit down for a minute. (*Lauren and her mom sit at the table, while Aunt Ziva pours herself a glass of orange juice.*) Last night I got a call from Grandpa. Grandma fell and broke her arm yesterday. They need our help, so Aunt Ziva and I are going to go see them today. We can't help them out *and* go see the hawks, too. I'm sorry, but it looks like you're going to miss the hawks again this year.

(*Lauren stares in disbelief at her mom before speaking.*)

LAUREN: (*her eyes tearing*) Is Grandma going to be all right?

Go On ▶

BETH: Yes. She was in some pain yesterday, but she's going to be fine.

LAUREN: We can't go next weekend?

BETH: I'm sorry, Lauren. You know how hard it is for me to get time off work.

20 AARON: (*thoughtfully, to Beth*) I bet I could help.

BETH: (*surprised*) Excuse me?

AARON: Whatever Grandma and Grandpa need help with today, I bet I could help …

LAUREN: (*catching on*) … instead of Aunt Ziva. And she and I could go help Grandma and Grandpa tomorrow, Mom, when you have to work …

AUNT ZIVA: … and Lauren and I can go to Corpus Christi to see the hawks today. It's no problem, really. I have the whole weekend off. And I'm sure Mom wouldn't want her favorite granddaughter—OK, her only granddaughter—to miss the hawk watch.

25 LAUREN: (*her face lighting up with hope*) Oh, Mom, please?

BETH: (*smiling*) Well, they say that <u>two heads are better than one</u>, and I guess your three heads are even better than that! I think it's a great idea.

LAUREN: I'll go get those binoculars for you, Aunt Ziva!

Go On ▶

42. As it is used in line 1, <u>adjust</u> means

    A. visit.

    B. make.

    C. judge.

    D. change.

43. Which BEST describes Scene 1 of the play?

    A. It introduces the characters.

    B. It hints at a conflict for Lauren.

    C. It suggests the theme of the drama.

    D. It explains Lauren's grandmother's injury.

44. As it is used in the description of the setting of Scene 2, what does <u>amusement</u> mean?

    A. not amused

    B. one who is amused

    C. capable of being amused

    D. the state of being amused

45. What do the stage directions within Scene 2 show about Aaron?

    A. He does not know what happened to his grandmother.

    B. He wants to go see the hawks in Corpus Christi.

    C. He knows something that he does not want to say.

    D. He is excited about something he wants to tell Lauren.

46. When Lauren says "don't take this the wrong way" to her mother in line 9, she means that

    A. she thinks her mother is lost.

    B. she doesn't want her mother to get upset.

    C. she sees that her mother is going to make a mistake.

    D. she believes that her mother is too sensitive.

Go On ▶

47. According to Lauren, how are the hawks like leaves?

    A. They are both fragile.

    B. They both ride on the wind.

    C. They both prefer warmer air.

    D. They fly or fall during the day.

48. When Beth says that "two heads are better than one" in line 26, she means that

    A. she wishes she had more than one head.

    B. Ziva should go with her to help their parents.

    C. the group thought of a better idea than she could.

    D. extra eyes are needed for watching the hawks.

49. What is the theme of the play?

    A. Things tend to turn out just as planned.

    B. A little imagination can solve a problem.

    C. Accept the things you cannot change.

    D. Bird watching is a fun hobby.

50. Using details from the play to support your answer, describe the relationship between Lauren and Aunt Ziva.

_____

_____

_____